Praise for *Ask Me for a Blessing (You Know You Need One)*

"What does blessing mean in the dirty, busy streets of a city? What does it mean for believers and nonbelievers, for the suffering and foolish and angry and afraid? In this beautifully real book, Adrian Dannhauser shows how the hands-on practice of public blessing invites everyone to see, to desire, and to become more."

—**Sara Miles**, author of *City of God: Faith in the Streets* and *Take This Bread: A Radical Conversion*

"If you're confused about what a blessing *is* and *does,* it's probably for good reason. These days, the word *blessing* is often reduced to a description of material wealth, cultural privilege, or just good luck. Got a new car for Christmas? You're #blessed. Celebrating thirty years of marriage? Well, then, count your #blessings. Adrian Dannhauser knows that sacred speech and spiritual conversations are too important to be handled without care. She understands that a blessing is more life-giving and more lifesaving than its popular usage. Dannhauser writes as someone who has spent years standing on the sidewalk of our culture, whispering good news to passing pedestrians. *Ask Me for a Blessing* is a much-needed renovation project for important spiritual ideas—blessing, yes, but also forgiveness, redemption, prayer, and even grace. What a gift!"

—**Jonathan Merritt**, contributing writer for *The Atlantic* and author of *Learning to Speak God from Scratch*

"Adrian Dannhauser removes the hashtag from the word *blessing* and returns all the grace, vulnerability, and love that a true blessing conveys. A nourishing book for everyone hungering for spiritual connection."

—**Sophfronia Scott**, author of *The Seeker and the Monk: Everyday Conversations with Thomas Merton*

"Beautifully written, unabashedly honest, *Ask Me for a Blessing* is a refreshingly humble reflection on the soul's ache for meaning. Like a late-night confessional among close friends, Adrian Dannhauser offers an intimate, compassionate, luminous reflection on the inner anxieties and struggles we all carry. I recommend this book to anyone seeking wisdom on the spiritual journey."

—**Mark Yaconelli**, author of *Between the Listening and the Telling: How Stories Can Save Us*

"Imagine walking down a busy New York sidewalk. You see a blackboard that says 'Ask Me for a Blessing.' Curious, you stop. A warmhearted and utterly approachable woman in a clergy collar listens to you and prays for you. You're so intrigued; you want to learn more, so you set up a lunch meeting. This book is like that conversation over lunch. You'll be (wait for it) blessed!"

—**Brian McLaren**, author of many books, including *Do I Stay Christian?*

"The world is starved for kindness. People are yearning to be heard. And the bulk of this population is not behind stained glass—they are in the streets. Through this beautiful book, we stand with Rev. Adrian Dannhauser as she courageously holds space in that pain, teaching us how to be present, vulnerable, and, most of all, a blessing."

—**Rev. Susan Sparks**, preacher, comedian, and author of *Laugh Your Way to Grace*

ASK ME FOR A BLESSING

Ask Me for a Blessing

(You know you need one)

ADRIAN DANNHAUSER

Broadleaf Books

Minneapolis

ASK ME FOR A BLESSING
(You Know You Need One)

Cover image: Illustration by James Kegley
Cover design: 1517 Media

Print ISBN: 978-1-5064-6804-4
eBook ISBN: 978-1-5064-6805-1

To the greatest blessings of my life,
Jess and Callaway

CONTENTS

FOREWORD

The New Testament Gospels remind us that although Jesus started his ministry in a house of worship—his hometown synagogue, no less—almost immediately he began to take his message to the streets. He shared his message with thousands at a time, on a mount and a plain, but also spoke one on one with individuals who wanted to go deeper and learn more. Some who heard Jesus remained obstinate, stuck in their own social or religious prejudices, and they responded to what he said with harsh criticism and even hostility. But countless others encountered him in the towns and along the road, heard his message of the way of love, of God's dream for this hurting and divided world, and accepted that message for what it was: a blessing!

It was the start of something remarkable, a movement that would continue through the centuries. That way of love, that dream of God, that blessing has passed from one person to another, as in a grand and glorious relay race. The way forward was not without its problems. Obstinate, hostile critics would continue to arise, often in the very institution that claimed to represent Jesus of Nazareth. Any honest recording of the church's history reveals crusades, inquisitions, pogroms, religious wars, and every kind of prejudice under the sun. But even in the darkest moments, key individuals would arise, some renowned and commemorated but many more known only by those persons whose lives they had blessed.

Now the baton has been passed to us. That way of love is resting in our hands to be shared through our words, through our actions. Want to know what I'm talking about? Then look no further than the pages that follow. Check out what Adrian Dannhauser has to say about the memorable encounters she has had with ordinary passersby, offering them a word of forgiveness or a listening ear, sharing the blessing that so many desperately need, though they may not even realize it until they receive it. The stories she relates are sometimes humorous and often poignant, and throughout all of them is the thread of human need, heartfelt connection, and divine love.

The book you hold in your hands is not some preachy textbook. In the various anecdotes that follow, Dannhauser beautifully unpacks the realities of blessing, forgiveness, and prayer, all the while reminding us that we really can be conduits of the love of God. After all, as the old English hymn puts it, "The saints of God are just folk like me, and I mean to be one too." Read on, and don't be surprised to find yourself truly blessed . . . and maybe even inspired to pass on a blessing to someone else you meet today.

—The Most Rev. Michael B. Curry,
Presiding Bishop of the Episcopal Church and
author of *Love Is the Way* and *The Power of Love*

1

HOW TO TOUCH THE HOLY

My church sits on Madison Avenue at 35th Street in New York City, one block from the Empire State Building and a five-minute walk to Grand Central Station. There are loads of passersby all day long. The vast majority of them don't venture inside the church, of course. But the constant foot traffic creates the perfect setup for an Episcopal priest with a penchant for chatting up strangers with an encouraging word.

Every Tuesday morning, I stand on the sidewalk right outside the church doors. I put on my vestments (a fancy name for the garb we wear in worship) and put out a chalkboard A-frame sign. It's the kind of sign that restaurants, bars, and coffee shops use to list the day's specials or display catchy phrases like "Rosé All Day" and "Congratulations! You made it out of bed." My catchy phrase is this: "Ask me for a blessing. God's grace is meant to be shared." I write it on the board, wipe the chalk dust from my hands, and then just kind of stand there. I try to look open and friendly but not overly eager or desperate. It's an art, really.

Over the next thirty minutes, most people will walk by me without making eye contact. Several will smile and nod or say good morning. Ten or so might actually stop and take me up on the offer of a blessing. All things considered, that's a pretty decent turnout. I suppose it doesn't hurt that New Yorkers tend to be bolder than most, as evidenced by the many questions I get. "Are you a nun?" is the most common. "Can I take your picture?" is a close second.

It's no surprise that many people don't know what to make of me and my "blessing booth," of sorts. I realize that the whole thing is weird to begin with, but especially for those who have little to no religious frame of reference. For years, an ongoing decline in religiosity has been reported by the Pew Research Center, Gallup, and Barna Group—leading organizations in providing in-depth research on faith and culture in America. According to all three, we live in an increasingly post-Christian country. More and more people identify as *nones*—those having no religious affiliation—or *dones*—those who once had a religious affiliation but no longer do.

And while plenty of cities are considered less religious than New York, I don't exactly live in a hot spot of religious observance. I was raised as a Southern Baptist in the Bible Belt, where it's unusual for someone *not* to be a Christian. In New York, however, I often feel like a missionary.

As such, I'm also not surprised that many (maybe most) people here aren't familiar with some basic religious symbols in mainline Christianity. The white clergy collar that fits tightly around my neck is a prime example. Once I was wearing my collar with a simple black clergy shirt while riding the subway. A stylishly dressed man took notice. "I *love* your shirt," he said. "It's just so . . . puritanical!" Turns out he was in fashion law (did you know that was a thing?) and wanted me to tell him the designer.

Many Christians don't recognize the significance of the collar either. A group of young women accosted me at a Chipotle one Sunday afternoon and said they were inviting new people to join their Bible study. They had no idea that the collar meant I was a minister—who, incidentally, had her own Bible study. I politely declined and complimented them on their faith and courage. It takes some serious boldness to invite strangers to join your Bible study.

It's a boldness I don't share. It's true that I look like a spectacle on the sidewalk and that I want to get people's attention. But I don't invite them to attend my church or any of our programs. Of course, if they ask about our worship services or ministries, I welcome them warmly. It's just not why I'm there. My goal is simply to be present with people for the sake of letting them know that God is present too. This happens through having conversation about life and God, praying with people who are open to that, and pronouncing God's blessing on everyone who asks for one.

It's all pretty low key, actually, and I've found that people really do want to talk about God. They have spiritual stories to share. They have burning questions. And some need to say they've been burned by the church but still love Jesus. These conversations are rare in our everyday lives. Religion is understood as a private matter and a taboo subject. But the need to give voice to our spiritual selves is percolating right there beneath the surface.

I've performed at a couple of open mic nights in New York City. I didn't sing or do stand-up. I simply told a story. It's a story about being chased by a gorilla in Africa and praying to God that the gorilla would get to somebody else before he got to me. It's a wild story, to be sure. Lots of drama as well as humor. The point, though, is that I spent most of my time onstage reflecting on prayer, human nature, sin, and redemption. After leaving the stage, strangers approached me, wanting to learn more and talk about their own experiences of God and Christianity. Because I'd outed myself as a person with some degree of spiritual substance, suddenly I'd created a safe space for them to turn to.

When I stand in front of my church once a week inviting people to ask me for a blessing, I create a safe space again. We need more spaces where we can have spiritual conversation. We need more people who offer us prayers and blessings. We need contexts in which we don't have to be embarrassed as we come to terms with our need for God. For this need will never go away, and it will never be filled by anything else. A full life cannot be lived without God in it. The good news is that God is already there. Whether you're wearing a clergy collar or aren't really sure what you believe about God, we can all help one another touch the holy.

》》》》》》》》》》》》

I got the idea for this ministry from Ashes to Go, a movement of sorts that involves taking church outside on Ash Wednesday. If you're not familiar with Ash Wednesday, it falls forty days before Easter and kicks off the church's season of Lent. Lent is a time for self-examination, repentance of sin, and recognition of our deep need for God. We focus on Jesus's self-sacrifice on the cross so we can more fully celebrate the joy of his resurrection.

In the process, we might give up something decadent that we really enjoy. In other words, we fast before we feast forty days later. And it all starts with receiving ashes on our foreheads as a symbol of our finitude in the face of God's vast and infinite love.

Even many Christians haven't heard of Ash Wednesday; growing up, I never did. But if you know about Mardi Gras, you can understand the concept. Live it up on Fat Tuesday before shifting spiritual gears the next morning. Of course, binge drinking isn't the only way to celebrate Fat Tuesday, which is traditionally known as Shrove Tuesday. Going back to the Middle Ages, on Shrove Tuesday, Christians would use up all the eggs, sugar, and fat—foods commonly forbidden during the Lenten fast—so they wouldn't go to waste. This meant pancakes for dinner, a tradition that continues in many churches and households today.

And don't forget bacon with those pancakes. You couldn't have meat during Lent either, which is the origin of the festival Carnival (Latin for "farewell to meat") in many Roman Catholic countries. One year, I, too, said farewell to meat for the season of Lent. This was a super-huge deal for a Southern girl whose favorite food is BBQ. I thought a big sacrifice would produce big results in my spiritual life, but the only result I remember is an iron deficiency. I tried to donate blood midway through Lent and was turned away with the instruction, "Go eat a hamburger and come back tomorrow."

When it comes to giving up something for Lent, I do much better with giving up a habit I want to break. Alternatively, I might take on a spiritual practice. Here's an example of both. Once a month, I meet with a spiritual director: a person, sometimes clergy and sometimes not, who has been trained to help people see God in their daily life. My current spiritual director is a Catholic sister. Before that, it was an Episcopal priest and professor. I once confessed to the priest-professor that I was getting into fights with people in my head—the driver who cut me off on the freeway or a family member who made a passive-aggressive comment during a phone call. I found myself stewing over this stuff. My spiritual director suggested I say the word *fast* every time I started to imagine giving someone a piece of my mind. It worked so well that I've been using this technique ever since. And those mental skirmishes have become few and far between . . . on a good day, at least.

No matter how you observe Lent, the point is to deepen your devotion to the divine. We strip away things that are unnecessary so that we can cleave to the one thing that matters: God. This is the message of Ash Wednesday. Someone, usually a clergyperson, will dip their thumb in ashes and then draw a small cross on your forehead while saying, "Remember that you are dust, and to dust you shall return." These words are based on Genesis 3:19, spoken by God to Adam when he and Eve had to leave the garden of Eden. They are a reminder that we all are sinners and we all will die. The ashes themselves are reminiscent of ashes that people in biblical times heaped on their heads as a sign of grief and repentance. Given this context, the act of receiving ashes might sound like a downer. But, in fact, the opposite is true.

For the countless Christians who observe Ash Wednesday, this ritual holds special appeal. Twice as many people come in my church on Ash Wednesday than on Easter Sunday. Why is that? I imagine part of the reason has to do with our location in Midtown

Manhattan. There are simply more people in the area on a weekday than on a Sunday. But there has to be more to it than that, and here's what I think is going on.

To remember that we are dust is to admit there is brokenness inside us. We all hurt, struggle, mess up, and fail. We all have a selfish streak, no matter how thick or thin that streak may be. We all get scared. No one has it all together, and that's okay. It's why we need God and why we need each other.

Then there's the physicality of it all. There is something so uniquely intimate about receiving ashes on your forehead, even from a stranger. The forehead is a tender spot, a place where human touch communicates kindness. A kiss on the forehead, whether it's romantic, platonic, or parental, is a demonstration of care. The same might be said when someone gently brushes their fingers across your forehead. I once surprised myself right before going under anesthesia for a surgery. I was scared and crying a little, so I asked the doctor to lightly stroke my forehead when I counted down from ten. I couldn't believe that I had let this request, which felt so juvenile, pop out of my mouth. But he honored it just the same. It was a brief moment of compassion that I will always remember.

When it comes to giving and receiving ashes, the care that's communicated comes from God. The person smudging that ashen cross on your forehead is mediating God's mercy and love. Most people probably don't think about this consciously, but it's undoubtedly what's taking place in that moment of spoken word and physical contact. And people love it, truly, madly, deeply. The draw to this ancient spiritual practice is evidence of a hunger for spiritual connection—a hunger that is felt not only in people of faith but also in society at large.

Responding to this hunger, clergy and laypeople alike have begun offering ashes on street corners and at train stations rather than confining this ritual to the interior of a church. Starting in seminary, I spent several Ash Wednesdays shivering outside in the dark hours of the morning, wearing fingerless gloves with my thumb caked in ashes. Throngs of people asked for ashes to go, eager to steal a sacred moment in the midst of their morning commute. *Remember that you are dust, and to dust you shall return.*

One year, at the recommendation of a clergy friend, I added an additional piece to the exchange. I started asking for the person's name and if they'd like me to pray for anything in particular. Some people had an answer on the tip of their tongue. "I hate my boss," blurted out one person. "My mother is in the hospital," said another. Other people pondered the question for a moment. "Hmmm . . . I want to be less selfish" (what a perfect one for Lent). However they came to it, nine times out of ten, people shared a prayer request. This gave me the opportunity to offer a brief prayer on the spot and then state the person's name before giving them ashes with the sacred reminder of their mortality. At first, I was amazed at how many people were receptive to having me pray for them. Life is hard, and we've all got stuff going on, but to be open about that on your way to work? And to a stranger wearing a robe?

Maybe I shouldn't have been so surprised. The felt need for spirituality is real. I see spirituality as connection to God, connection to others, and connection to self. While organized religion isn't a necessary part of the equation, it can certainly help. Yet there's no denying that religious affiliation and connection to God has decreased among Americans over the years. There's also no denying that feelings of loneliness and social isolation have risen, especially as people spend less time together in face-to-face interaction. While technology can help people preserve or increase social connections, it can also lead some individuals to feel more alone and with a sense that they don't belong. This, in turn, can affect a person's connection to self, especially if it results in depression.

The point is that these three prongs of spirituality are interwoven. The simple act of offering ashes captures all of them: an experience of God, an experience with another person, and an experience of inner reflection. Add in intercessory prayer, in which one person prays for the other, and all three forms of connection increase, sometimes dramatically.

If so many people wanted prayer when they came for ashes, I thought, maybe I would get a similar reaction with offering blessings. Giving someone a blessing involves the same motion, after all, just without the ashes and with different words. When I bless someone,

I draw a cross on the person's forehead with my thumb and say, "The blessing of God Almighty, Father, Son, and Holy Spirit, be upon you and remain with you always."

I started getting excited at the prospect of giving out blessings instead of ashes. I pulled out my chalkboard sign, and instead of writing "Ashes to Go," I wrote "Blessings to Go." I stared at this message for a minute, a bit unsatisfied, and then erased it in favor of something much better: "Ask me for a blessing. God's grace is meant to be shared."

I set up in front of the church, and as expected, people stopped, and the prayer requests followed. In each case, I offered a prayer for the specific need expressed. Then I closed by saying the person's name and pronouncing words of blessing while making the sign of the cross on their forehead.

>>>>>>>>>>>>

Five years later, I'm still at it. During this time, I've blessed hundreds of people from all walks of life, recorded video messages for those who wanted me to speak directly to their loved ones, conversed with a number of atheists (one of whom now attends my church), and defended my ministry to people who frown upon it. "So *this* is what the church has come to?" a man once asked me sarcastically.

Frankly, it's what the church has already been up to. Otherwise, it wouldn't be here. God calls us to minister in the marketplace, to preach in the public square, to witness in ways that feel a little uncomfortable or even a little crazy. Even Christians who shy away from talking about their faith with strangers, or talking about their faith at all, can appreciate the reasons why others feel an urgency to proclaim it. At its foundation, Christianity recognizes a God who offers grace unmerited in a world where we think we have to earn our way. The body of Christ, as expressed in Christian community, offers human touch and connection in a world where we are increasingly alienated from one other. Following the teachings of Jesus offers meaning and purpose in a world where people often feel they don't matter or can't truly make a difference. My response to that sarcastic man? I'm just keeping tradition alive, bro.

While this ministry has come to feel natural to me, others have found it remarkable. I've been interviewed for the nightly news, photographed for someone's art show, featured on podcasts, and profiled by an international news agency. That's how this book came about. My editor read about "Ask me for a blessing" in an article online. The notoriety is nice, but aside from the occasional New Yorker who says they saw me on the five o'clock news, it hasn't changed anything. My ministry has remained pretty consistent, as have people's prayer requests. The specifics vary, of course, but I've noticed some themes: a sick friend, a struggling child, an upcoming job interview, the need for more peace and less stress, the state of our nation or our world. Half of those who stop are in crisis. Someone always cries. A few are simply curious or just looking for a good way to start the day.

One of my earliest encounters was with a woman who looked quizzically at my sign and asked, "What's a blessing?" She said she'd never had any exposure to religion and was very intrigued. "Well, a blessing is a pronouncement of God's goodness while also being a request for God's favor or protection," I told her. "It's a type of prayer." She cocked her head to the side. I took a deep breath and, before I lost my nerve, said, "Do you need a prayer? Maybe for yourself or a loved one?"

For the next several weeks, the woman brought a multitude of prayer requests. Her father's health was failing. Her family life felt hectic and disjointed, with everyone pulled in different directions. A friend's daughter was cutting herself. Each week we prayed, and each week the look of curiosity on her face lessened. She became more earnest than inquisitive. A sign of faith, perhaps?

Then her work situation changed, and I haven't seen her since. I don't know if this woman has made it to church or opened a Bible, and I don't know whether she will ever do either of these things. But I would guess she's offered a prayer or two—and hopefully several. Prayer is a fitting introduction to faith. More often than not, life's difficulties are what drive us to God. And approaching God from a place of need is one of the most faithful postures we can take.

Not long after meeting this woman who asked me to define *blessing*, someone else posed a very different question: "Aren't we supposed to *be* a blessing?" My heart nearly burst. "Yes!" I exclaimed, probably a little too loudly. "As God told Abraham, you are blessed to be a blessing!" This is a point I'm constantly driving home with my congregation, and especially with children when I lead them in service projects for those struggling with homelessness. Like all of us, children grapple with why some people have so much and some have so little. Are the rich more blessed than the poor? Perhaps the best response to that question comes from a child in my church: "My family is so rich. We have everything we need and people who love us."

But while simple answers are often the best answers, the underlying questions keep us restless. What does it mean to be blessed, and are some people more blessed than others? And where does grace come in? When I write on my chalkboard sign "God's grace is meant to be shared," in my mind, this means the grace that shows up when two or three are gathered in Christ's name. It always feels like a little trinity when someone stops to speak with me: the person, me, and the Holy Spirit swirling around us.

Of course, an important part of this ministry—for some people, at least—is the fact that I'm an ordained minister. Many people who want a blessing from me put great stock in being blessed by a priest. To some, I represent the institutional church—fair enough. To others, I represent God—which feels crazy weird and like a lot of pressure. And other people assume I must be super-spiritual—kind of like when I ask my mom to pray for me because she's a person of deep faith. "The prayer of a righteous person is powerful and effective."

Honestly, I don't know that my clergy status should matter all that much. But I'm frequently reminded that it does, especially when non-English speakers stop for a blessing after they see me make the sign of the cross on someone else's forehead. We can't communicate with words, but we both know it's a blessing they want. It's a testament to the power of this ancient ritual. Blessing is a shared religious practice that transcends human language and reaches across countless generations and cultures.

And that brings me to another definition of *blessing*: God reaching through us to touch another person. This is what my ministry is all about and why I am blessed in it. "Ask me for a blessing" creates a space to touch the holy and for the holy to touch us. It's a need many people don't even realize they have, a need that is heightened by today's epidemic of loneliness and our society's weakening connection to God. For all the wonders of modern technology, there's no substitute for in-person interaction. And there's certainly no substitute for relationship with the divine. Fortunately, the appeal of blessing remains strong—as a curiosity to some, a tangible form of grace to others, and a brief connection between two strangers that is unlike anything else.

Sometimes people use the word *evangelism* to describe what I'm doing out there on the sidewalk on Tuesday mornings. It's a word that makes some people—both Christians and others—shudder, with images of people shouting "Jesus saves!" through a bullhorn on street corners, carrying signs that warn of eternal damnation, passing out tracts that lay out five easy steps to salvation, or accosting strangers with the question, "If you were to die tonight, *where would you go?*" These methods are grounded in the theological belief that only Christians are going to heaven. It's not a belief I share. But even if I did, I wouldn't be about scaring people into confessing Jesus as Lord.

To me, evangelism is simply about speaking the truth of God's grace, love, and mercy into people's lives. Conversion is never the point. Blessing is. And while I definitely evangelize in the pulpit—preaching is about proclaiming the good news, after all—my favorite context for evangelism is personal interaction. This can include conversation, prayer, or conversation that leads to prayer.

Offering a blessing is surprisingly simple yet powerful beyond measure, for it simultaneously extends an invitation to another person and an invitation to God to move in that person's life. This is where grace abounds. Grace from God that is meant to be shared. As I am fed in this ministry, may you be fed by this book and come to know the God who is ready and waiting to show up for you.

2

THAT AMORPHOUS THING CALLED *GRACE*

I'm a fan of real talk. Pleasantries can be an important warm-up to meaningful conversation, but let's not stop with comments about the weather and where we're from. And, please, no beating around the bush. Perhaps this is why I like talking with people about how they relate to God. The conversation never stays surface level for long. If you find me at a cocktail party, I'm much more likely to be sitting in a corner talking to someone about the pros and cons of our religious upbringings than working the room.

Real talk is also why I like prayer and particularly praying with other people. I know that might sound strange. The idea of praying with another person freaks some people out or at least makes them feel vulnerable, whether they're the one offering the prayer or the one being prayed for. It's much less intimidating to tell someone "You're in my prayers"—and then wait until we're alone to offer those prayers to God (if we remember, that is). But whether you're with someone or by yourself, the great thing about prayer is that we can let go of pretense. Prayer cuts through all our superficiality. It slices right down to the heart of getting real about our faults, frailties, and need for God, with whom there is no fronting.

If you're like me, spiritual conversation (which is real talk *about* God) and prayer (which is real talk *to* God) often go hand in hand. Same goes for spiritual conversation and cocktail parties. And while it's admittedly rare to have all three converge, that's sort of what happened when someone asked me for a [bleeping] blessing.

I usually offer blessings in front of my church on Tuesday mornings, near the end of rush hour, when people are still heading to work. But occasionally I'll set up my "Ask me for a blessing" sign somewhere else, like my neighborhood's annual street fair. The fair involves

New York City closing off five or six blocks along Park Avenue. People have the chance to meander, hear some live music, stop at food trucks, browse a small selection of items for sale, and learn about various community organizations.

So one year, since my church is part of the community, I wedged myself and my "Ask me for a blessing" sign between two booths in the middle of the fair. The local neighborhood association had a booth on my right, and some group selling used books was on my left. Not the most exciting attractions, I thought, but maybe I'd still get some business.

In fact, my ho-hum neighbors made me stick out even more. I didn't exactly blend into the background. Without the church behind me, lending some legitimacy to my operation, my vestments felt like a costume. They were also hot as hell in ninety-degree weather. "I like your scarf," said the woman selling books. "But aren't you hot?" She was talking about my stole, which is a long, skinny piece of fabric that many Christian clergy wear around their necks and that hangs down in front on either side. Mine was green silk embroidered with gold thread—very pretty, ornate, traditional, and definitely not used for warmth. I found her comment amusing, but it also made me feel self-conscious. Why had I chosen to wear my full get-up, including a white floor-length robe—and, consequently, a beet-red face? I was a total sideshow.

Perhaps the sideshow vibe was a good thing because lots of people stopped by—way more than I normally get during the weekday commute—and they all were in a good mood. Two in particular were in a *great* mood. They were women in their twenties and clearly day drinking—prepartying for an evening event, as I came to find out. As they got close enough to see my sign, one of them said quite loudly to her friend, "I *need* a [bleeping] blessing." Fill in the bleep.

I yelled out, "Come on over!" and immediately questioned my decision to beckon someone drunk enough to modify *blessing* with an expletive. But too late. These ladies were already standing in front of me, wondering how exactly I might fit into their street fair experience.

They ended up being receptive to, or at least humored by, my explanation of this ministry. So when I asked them for prayer requests, the one who had expressed her need for a blessing told me the guy she liked was "being an a**hole." Matters of the heart can be so hard. I had a feeling this person was stringing her along, in *her* mind at least.

"Maybe we should pray that he grows up and starts treating you with a little more respect," I said. "Is that right?" It was right. This young woman kept talking about this young man, her feelings, and their relationship—or, more precisely, lack thereof. Everyone knows that unrequited love sucks. Possibly worse is love that's requited to some extent but not enough to leave you feeling safe and secure in a committed relationship. I'm far removed from this feeling after many years of marriage, but I can still remember it. And I can remember hating how much a certain guy who was only sort of into me occupied my thoughts, while also indulging those thoughts and therefore doing nothing to get him out of my mind.

I gave her an empathetic look and nodded as she expressed her frustration—with him, with herself. After every couple of sentences, I would essentially paraphrase what she said in the form of a prayer, so the whole exchange stayed conversational. At first, she had been lighthearted about the whole thing. Midway through, she was crying and emphatic in describing the unfairness of her situation. By the end, her tears of hurt were mixed with tears of comfort. I closed with a blessing and an affirmation about God's love for her.

When we were finished, the young woman dried her eyes, let out a big cathartic sigh, and said, "I liked that blessing." Her friend gave her a little pat on the back. Then they linked arms and staggered off through the fair.

What strikes me in thinking back on this encounter is how honest and incredibly direct this young woman was. Perhaps because she'd been drinking, perhaps not. I know nothing of her spiritual background, but I wonder if she ever feels the freedom to be that candid with God in prayer. Most of us can easily talk about our problems to other people. But how often do we do that with God? How often do we give it to God straight?

Not often enough, from what I've seen. One prayer request I frequently get is for direction from God. Someone is at a crossroads: not sure whether to stay in a relationship, for example, or just feeling stuck or confused by life circumstances. "I just need God to show me what to do, and I'll do it!" There's a sense of desperation in this plea.

I know what to pray for in this situation—God's guidance, sensitivity to the movement of the Holy Spirit, the courage to step out in faith. But if the person seems to have the time and inclination for a longer conversation, I'll go deeper. "When have you felt God guide you in the past?" I'll ask. "How do you think God feels about your situation?" Or sometimes even, "What's your prayer life like?"

A common response to that last question is this: "I don't want to bother God with my problems. God has more important things to do." Now this can easily be a cop-out. It's no secret that the more we invest in our relationship with God, the better we'll be able to sense where God is leading us. Not wanting to bother God is often an excuse for not bothering to pray.

But that's not always the case. I've met plenty of faithful Christians who serve God and love neighbor yet show signs of spiritual anorexia. They have difficulty receiving God's love and grace, which is spiritual food. They might fear being a burden to God, being less than perfect, or having needs of any kind. The result is a resistance to being divinely nurtured and nourished.

I once stumbled across this saying I've grown to love: "Have you prayed about it as much as you've talked about it?" Raise your hand if the answer is no. I'll join you. We assume God knows what we're going through—and, of course, God does. But God wants to be bothered. God wants to be called upon. God wants the chance to meet our deepest needs.

When I was trying to come up with a title for this book, I did an experiment. I changed the wording on my chalkboard sign from "Ask me for a blessing. God's grace is meant to be shared." to "Ask me for a blessing. God knows you need one." It made a difference. More people stopped than usual, and I got lots of smiles and chuckles from those humored by the new message. It captures the extent of our need with a dose of exasperation. The good Lord knows we're all just muddling our way through.

Then there was one person who truly took the message to heart. She was a psychotherapist, and the first thing out of her mouth was "I have trouble asking God for what I need." She proceeded to talk about the demands of her practice, how much her patients depended on her, and the heavy weight of responsibility on her shoulders. I could relate. We are both in helping professions that require us to be strong so that other people can become vulnerable. Even when I feel depleted, it can be tempting to hold on to the "I must stay strong" attitude at all times and at all costs. It can be difficult to acknowledge my own weakness for fear that I'll let somebody down or not live up to my own (usually unrealistic) expectations. Yet God didn't create us to be self-sufficient. God created us to find fulfillment, joy, and a sense of sustained serenity that's only available through letting our guard down and letting God in.

All of us—people of faith and people of no faith alike—are hungry for God's grace. We're all hungry for spiritual connection to the divine because, intuitively, we know there has to be more than this. There's more to life than what we see. And there's more to us than what we've done—good, bad, or ugly. The first step is to acknowledge the hunger. Grace begins when we recognize the need for more than what the world offers and what we can offer ourselves.

>>>>>>>>>>>>>

Okay, then. What exactly *is* grace? What is this amorphous thing that we crave?

The Episcopal *Book of Common Prayer* defines grace as "God's favor toward us, unearned and undeserved; by grace God forgives our sins, enlightens our minds, stirs our hearts, and strengthens our wills." It's a helpful definition, and there's lots to unpack, beginning with *unearned and undeserved favor.* This is something God offers to us, but it's also something we can offer one another. So let's start there.

One late-November day, a middle-aged woman approached me with tears in her eyes. Before I even opened my mouth, she said with all the strength she could muster, "My husband left me last year because he's gay. Thanksgiving will be the first time I'm having him back in the house."

Wow. I could tell she was gearing up emotionally, trying to put on a brave face while also revealing a mix of heartache, anger, and compassion. Holidays are charged enough as it is without the added stress of a strained relationship. I was impressed by this olive branch she was extending and even more by her marked determination to extend it.

Was it forgiveness she was offering? Yes and no. She didn't fault her husband for leaving, but she was hurt just the same. In a sense, the grace she offered was about her own healing: refusing to live with the emotional weight of bitterness and disappointment. This woman also offered the grace of reconciliation. She wanted to remain in a relationship with her soon-to-be ex-husband, even though that relationship would look drastically different going forward. I imagine he was extending some grace to her too.

Acts of grace aren't always easy. Some flow naturally, but some require grit. Like the grace and grit of the cross. Christians believe that through the cross, Jesus mended the breach between humanity and God that was created by sin. He was tempted to turn away from his mission, but his love for a world that rebelled against him ultimately won out. On the cross, Jesus brought all of humanity into his loving embrace, declaring that

God wants a relationship with us that is intimate and eternal. We believe this is the ultimate example of God's saving grace and our model of reconciliation. Grace and grit: it's the motto of Jesus, the prophets, the martyrs, and those who invite exes to the dinner table.

Let's return to the definition of *grace* to see what other shape God's favor can take. The *Book of Common Prayer* says that grace "enlightens our minds, stirs our hearts, and strengthens our wills." When I think of grace enlightening my mind, I think of gaining fresh insights into Scripture, seeing other people and the world as God sees them, and discovering my blind spots in terms of prejudice and privilege, implicit bias, and sins I didn't even realize I was committing. Grace has stirred my heart to compassion as well as repentance, acts of kindness, and a deeper commitment to follow Jesus. It can also give me a visceral sense of the Holy Spirit. There are times when you find your heart "strangely warmed," as John Wesley famously said. Or, to quote my dear old dad, "You know the Holy Spirit is all around, but sometimes you can feel it sock you right in the gut." And then there is grace that strengthens the will, whether that be the will to resist temptation or the will to get the job done, especially jobs given to us by God.

These are but a few examples, and I'm sure you can think of more. I imagine you've offered prayers—for yourself, loved ones, and maybe enemies too—asking for God to enlighten minds, stir hearts, and strengthen wills in some form or fashion.

For me, the most basic prayer of this variety is "God, help me do my best." This is a prayer I've offered up on a regular basis for as long as I can remember. It harkens back to childhood, with memories of tests, dance recitals, and sports.

So far in this ministry, I've had only one sports-related prayer request. It came from a man who coached a middle-school boys' basketball team. They had a big game coming up that Saturday, and he was feeling nervous about it. "It can't hurt to pray, right?" he asked me when he stopped by one Tuesday morning. Right. Before getting down to business, we spent a few minutes bonding over our love for, and true fascination with, middle schoolers. He talked about their exaggerated, hormone-induced emotions and how fun it is to watch his team explode into laughter or shock over the smallest thing. I told him how I marvel at the ability of middle schoolers in my congregation to think deeply and act maturely while also making fart noises and not using napkins when they eat. And, of course, we both spoke to the experience of adolescents placing us on a pedestal one minute and making us the butt of a joke the next. Middle schoolers are gangly and goofy, enthusiastic yet too cool for school, and they want to make you proud.

This coach was proud indeed and 100 percent invested in his boys' growth and success—not only as basketball players but as strong yet vulnerable and endearingly ridiculous teenagers on their way to becoming young men. I commented that coaching must be a form of ministry for him. His eyes started to well up. He nodded vigorously and let out an embarrassed laugh.

This loss of composure clearly caught him off guard, which made it even more touching. He turned his head away to discreetly wipe away a tear. Then he cleared his throat, widened his stance, and bowed his head. "Just pray that they kick some a** this weekend," he said in a deep voice.

I prayed that they would leave it all on the court. Not that I'm opposed to using the word *a*** in a prayer. My philosophy is that curse words are to be used sparingly, only when needed to convey extra-intense emotions, never directed at another person, and never as a syntactic crutch when a better word will do. Prayer is the perfect place to bring intense emotions, especially if it's an emotion you want God to help you move past. When it comes to kicking *a*** in a sports game, I just don't like praying for one team to win over the other. It presupposes that someone on the other side could offer the same prayer and cancel out your own. Plus, I'm all about praying for God's help to do our best, remember?

In any event, the coach seemed satisfied with my prayer. As we said our goodbyes, I silently thanked God for how deeply this man cared for his team. It reminded me of the loving care I have for my own child, which is a small glimpse into the vastness of God's love for us. God created us for no other reason but love. Parents have children purely to love and delight in them. To learn who they are, cultivate their character, and support their flourishing. Like coaching, parenthood is not about what the child can do for the parents but what the parents do for the child.

Of course, not all parents are this emotionally mature all the time, and we know that family dysfunction abounds. But when parents do rise to the occasion, the best of their human loving is a window into God's love for humankind. God loves us beyond measure, and much like that basketball coach or a proud parent, God gets teary-eyed just thinking about our efforts to do the right thing, even when we fail. Does this mean we always do our best? Definitely not. But God is always for us, cheering us on. Perhaps even rooting for us to kick some a**.

>>>>>>>>>>>

People often come to me seeking approval. They usually begin with a lengthy explanation of a personal problem. I can tell they want me to validate their feelings, which I normally do. Then sometimes they want my permission to take a certain action. This could be anything from taking antidepressants, to taking back a cheating partner, to taking a new job. While some people are just looking for a little spiritual input, others clearly want my stamp of approval—or, more accurately, God's stamp of approval and the imprimatur of the church.

I'm wary of picking up that stamp, especially after a five-minute conversation on the sidewalk with someone I've just met. But there are times when I reach for it right away. "Is it okay to be gay?" Yes! Stamp. "Is it okay to divorce my abusive spouse?" Yes! Stamp.

And the question that underlies so many others: "Does God still love me?" Yes! Double stamp.

This goes to the heart of grace as a manifestation of God's love. We may anger or sadden God on occasion, but the love of our Creator, who brought us into being, is always there. God's favorable disposition—of a parent to a child—is always there. The truth of this statement is easy to tout but often difficult to internalize. It's hard to receive God's love. It's hard to accept God's approval. I see people struggle with it all the time.

We can be so quick to make God's love conditional, contingent on how we behave. Whenever I see that lie rear its ugly head, I seek to correct it on the spot. But I know there's more to it than that. Even if the person connects with the great mercy and love of God in the moment, feelings of unworthiness can creep back in later. Receiving God's love takes time and intention; it's a practice.

For me, this requires being still for ten minutes a day and focusing on my love for God and God's love for me. If I'm feeling really disciplined, I'll do this practice in the church, which is a short walk from both my home and my office. I sit in a pew, breathe deeply, and bring my attention to my heart to help me feel the love I share with God.

More often, I'm too lazy to walk over to the church (pathetic, I know), and half the time I don't even sit up at all. I lie down like I would after finishing a yoga class—on the floor, in my bed, on the couch—with feet slightly apart, arms by my side, and palms facing upward. Then I think of the love of God being poured into my heart through the Holy Spirit. I imagine there's this great pitcher of liquid love that never ends. When I drift away from this practice and don't spend sufficient time with God, my desire for love, attention, and approval from others increases. It's not a good feeling. I'd much rather God fill those longings.

And God does, beginning with the ultimate stamp of approval most clearly seen in the sacrament of holy baptism. Baptism is a tangible means of receiving grace, so bear with me as we go back to the classroom for a moment. According to the *Book of Common Prayer*, sacraments are "outward and visible signs of an inward and spiritual grace." The outward sign in baptism is the water, in which a person is baptized in the name of the Father, and of the Son, and of the Holy Spirit. The inward and spiritual grace is "union with Christ in his death and resurrection, birth into God's family the Church, forgiveness of sins, and new life in the Holy Spirit." That's a lot, I know. Is baptism required to receive these things: union with Christ, rebirth, forgiveness, and new life? No, they are all forms of God's unmerited favor. God's grace cannot be denied to anyone; human action or inaction isn't the final word. But baptism does create a conduit for receiving grace in our lives if we choose to make use of it.

Think of the difference between picking up sand with a cup versus using your hand. If you use your hand, it's not so easy. The sand spills over; the grains run through your fingers. You're not left with all that much.

But if you have a cup, you can scoop the sand right up. Baptism is the cup. It's a spiritual vessel, a means for receiving grace made available to us through Christ, and it's up to the Christian whether to use this gift.

In my Christian denomination, something really special follows the sacrament of baptism. The priest uses holy oil blessed by a bishop to make the sign of the cross on the person's forehead while saying, "You are sealed by the Holy Spirit in baptism and marked as Christ's own forever." This sealing is a sign of God's promise to never let us go. God approves of us even when God doesn't approve of what we're doing. God loves us even when we're unlovable. God's seal of approval means that we are forever sealed in relationship with God. It's a reminder "that neither death, nor life, nor angels, nor rulers, nor things present, nor things to come, nor powers, nor height, nor depth, nor anything else in all creation, will be able to separate us from the love of God in Christ Jesus our Lord."

When I pronounce God's blessing over someone and make the sign of the cross on their forehead, I think of that seal. I acknowledge God's imprint on that individual. The person standing in front of me is, like all of us are, made in God's image. I remember that God created humankind and saw that it was good. Loved. Blessed. And approved.

>>>>>>>>>>>>

I once had two women back to back tell me they stopped attending church over a decade ago. One had returned recently, and one was still staying away, although she was flirting with the idea of coming back. Neither told me why she had left, but both mentioned they were raised Catholic. They also mentioned a fondness, and even a yearning, for the Holy Eucharist: bread and wine consecrated by a priest as the body and blood of Christ. The sacrament of the Eucharist, also called Communion or the Lord's Supper, is a means of grace in my tradition as well.

Remember the part about sacraments being outward and visible signs of inward and spiritual grace? In the Eucharist, the bread and the wine are the outward signs; Christ's body and blood are the inward grace. To get a little more specific, that wine-soaked wafer is literally spiritual food infused with the real presence of Jesus. It's what I like to call "edible grace." It strengthens our union with Christ and helps us to follow him as disciples.

When I was speaking with the two women about their desire to receive the Eucharist, I told each of them that being away from church for an extended period of time meant suffering from "Eucharistic famine." I'd picked up this term from a Catholic sister and seminary professor, Dr. Janet Ruffing.

I once heard Dr. Ruffing make the argument that Catholic clergy should be allowed to marry for pastoral reasons. There aren't enough priests in Latin America and Africa, which are places where the Catholic Church is growing. This priest shortage is resulting in what she calls Eucharistic famine because Catholics in these areas don't have ready access to the sacraments. I hadn't known about this problem before, and I agree that allowing Catholic clergy to marry—or be women!—would help solve it.

In any event, it got me thinking of all the Christians closer to home who *do* have ready access to the Eucharist but aren't partaking. They are essentially on a self-imposed fast from the most important spiritual food. Of course, there are many Christians who don't observe the Eucharist in the first place. I didn't have it growing up. In fact, I could probably count on my fingers how many times I took Communion during my entire childhood. But I still developed a strong and passionate faith and felt the nearness of God—in worship, the arts, nature, prayer. Most of all, I felt, and still feel, God in fun that is truly carefree and characterized by a sense of joyful abandon.

God's grace extends way beyond the Eucharist. But for those who find comfort and nourishment in this spiritual practice, forgoing it creates a real longing for experiencing the nearness of God in a particular way.

A dear and hilarious friend once told me, "If I don't get that body [of Christ], my week starts to get all funky." That about sums it up for me. Some people would say the same thing about attending a church service, whether or not it includes receiving the Eucharist. Some people would say the same thing about reading their Bible, going to God in daily prayer, or even having a nightly cup of chamomile tea.

While the church has a certain understanding of the sacraments—baptism and Eucharist being the big two because they were instituted by Jesus—it also has a history of finding God's grace all around us, uncontained by ritual. One of my favorite poems is "The Sacraments" by St. Francis of Assisi from the early thirteenth century:

I once spoke to my friend, an old squirrel, about the
Sacraments—he got so excited

and ran into a hollow in his tree and came
back holding some acorns, an owl feather,
and a ribbon he found.

And I just smiled and said, "Yes dear,
you understand:

everything imparts His grace."

According to St. Francis, pretty much any material thing can be a vehicle for grace. This divine materiality makes sense in a religion that proclaims God became incarnate in a human body.

I often say that I'm not spiritual enough to *not* have some physicality to my faith. I pray with a wooden cross that fits neatly into the palm of my hand. I light candles and breathe in essential oils. These are my acorns and feathers. And if they can impart God's grace, we as humans certainly can too.

>>>>>>>>>>>>

A few years ago, I was walking near Herald Square, always a busy area of Manhattan, and came upon a group of people wearing red aprons. Printed on the back was the message "Prayer changes things." I had seen this sight before in another part of the city, so I knew right away these folks were out there to pray with and for anyone passing by. The aprons come from Prayer Stations, a ministry that provides supplies and training for Christians to offer intercessory prayer for people walking down the street or in any outdoor public space.

I was rushing to an appointment, but I still stopped for prayer. I was excited to be on the receiving end of a prayer ministry similar to mine. Moreover, I needed it. I'd recently learned that my grandfather was actively dying, and I'd just planned a trip back home to say goodbye.

The person I stopped to pray with turned out to be a Baptist pastor from Indiana. I told him about my grandfather, how sad I was to be losing him, and how I was a bit nervous to officiate at his funeral when the time came. The pastor gave me a word of advice: use my grandfather's first name (not "Papa") throughout the service to make sure I didn't get so choked up that I couldn't talk. Then he held my hand and prayed a very simple prayer.

Many of the things I observe and hear from people in my own street prayer ministry became true for me. I cried. I thought how this was just what I needed right when I needed it, and God must have known that. I felt strengthened, spiritually nourished, and a little readier to deal with what lay ahead. There is no better word to describe my experience than *grace*. Nothing but grace.

At the end of the day, *grace* is a term that remains amorphous. Even the most spiritually mature and theologically advanced among us continue to puzzle at the meaning of God's grace: unmerited favor, forgiveness of sin, spiritual food, God's love made manifest, divine influence running through our lives. Nothing quite captures the fullness of the term. There is no way to distill it without explaining away the mystery.

But I can attest to the grace I witness as I stand on the sidewalk and talk with strangers. Tears are a sign that grace is unearned and a true act of God's mercy. Gratitude, and sometimes wonderment, at the experience of God's love is a sign of spiritual hunger satisfied. Peace, strength, resolve, and joy are signs of God's nearness and ongoing presence. The grace I witness looks and feels like the gift that it is. It's what we all long for, and it's the blessing God longs to give.

3

MORE THAN A HASHTAG

"When I count my blessings, I count you twice!" It was one of my parishioners. She is a petite fireball with big hair and an even bigger personality, and she sports a different manicure every time I see her. Always on the go, she had just rushed past me while I stood by my sign on the sidewalk. Then she turned for a little backward jog as she pointed a glittery nail at me to make her point. I count her as a blessing too, both in my life and in the life of the church. There's no doubt she enlivens both.

Counting our blessings—offering prayers of thanksgiving to God—is an important spiritual practice. The

Bible teaches, and I truly believe, that everything good in our lives is connected to God. Everything good in our lives is a gift from God, whether it's a relationship, a high IQ, or a 401K. To quote one of my favorite verses of Scripture, "Every generous act of giving, with every perfect gift, is from above, coming down from the Father of lights." Beautiful, right?

I thank God freely and frequently, but here's where it starts to get tricky. I have trouble getting on board with #blessed. This hashtag is one we see all over the place and used with all kinds of photos, from new cars to new babies to beautiful vacation spots. Technically, it's a form of counting one's blessings, just on social media.

And what's wrong with counting one's blessings on social media? Nothing, I suppose, as long as we don't locate our blessedness in our own actions. As long as we recognize that we don't have this blessing because of our own wisdom or excellence or righteousness. As long as we really are expressing gratitude for the ways in which God's hand has been at work in our lives. After all, a blessing has to come from outside of us. I can't bless myself.

My problem is not about a hashtag any more than it's about the specific blessing attached to it. I'm just wary of using #blessed as a prayer of thanksgiving to God when so many others use it as a way to point to themselves, as in "Look at this great stuff God has given me . . . Look at this great stuff . . . Look at me!"

In contrast, the truest form of gratitude to God has humility at its heart. I learned this lesson from a man in remission from cancer. My church is quite close to a major hospital, so many of the people who ask me for a blessing are on their way to visit patients or are patients themselves. He was headed to the hospital for a CT scan to make sure the cancer hadn't come back. We prayed that everything would be clear, and he told me about his journey.

He'd received the diagnosis in his thirties, when he was in the best shape of his life. This news came as a total shock, as did the intensity of suffering that followed. He spoke about being humbled by the cancer itself, how chemotherapy and radiation literally brought him to his knees in physical pain and weakness. So much of his life felt ripped away. Yet this was what allowed him to experience another type of humility—a humility in response to the outpouring of graciousness and generosity from all the people surrounding him. The level of support took him by surprise.

He reminded me of someone who receives an award for a major achievement and is visibly shocked when their name is called. Then, in the acceptance speech, they talk about how humbled they are to be receiving such an honor. I'm sure I've seen dozens of actors do this during the Oscars, and I never quite understood it. Humbled by an award?

But hearing this cancer survivor describe the various ways he'd received love and support from family, friends, and people he barely knew brought it together for me. He was describing a feeling of undeservedness mixed with immense gratitude. This mix of emotions is something we can feel in the face of great honor and also in the face of great pardon. I asked the cancer survivor if this was the humility he was talking about, if the humility he felt was akin to being humbled by the gift of God's grace. "Exactly," he said. Exactly. We can be humbled by our limitations and experiences of human frailty (cancer being one of them) in the same way that we can be humbled by God's infinite majesty. "Humble yourselves before the Lord," as we read in the book of James. But even more than that, even more than being humbled by God's greatness, we're humbled by the greatness of God's love for us. A divine love most fully demonstrated by Jesus in his death on the cross.

Something tells me that #blessed doesn't quite capture this humility for most people, especially when I see it emblazoned on T-shirts and jewelry and all manner of merchandise, including my daughter's pencil case for seventh grade. At the same time, there's some truth to that hashtag, regardless of the disposition of the heart of the person using it. My daughter is too young to experience a deep spiritual humility, but she is undeniably blessed in that she's fortunate in a variety of ways: smart, beautiful, talented, wants for nothing. (Yes, I'm biased as a mother, but that doesn't make me wrong.)

And here's where our understanding of blessing gets even trickier. We can't help but compare ourselves to other people in determining just how blessed we are. Have you ever uttered, or at least thought, "There but for the grace of God go I"? This familiar saying is attributed to John Bradford, a major figure of the Protestant Reformation in England, which flourished under King Edward and then took a major hit when Queen Mary assumed the throne. Mary tried to restore the country to Catholicism and papal justice, so she had Bradford imprisoned in the Tower of London for his role in the Reformation. The year was 1553, and during his imprisonment, Bradford looked out the window one day to see a group of criminals being led to the scaffold for public execution. He said aloud, "There but for the grace of God goes John Bradford." Ironically, there indeed went Bradford two years later, when he burned at the stake on charges of heresy.

Bradford's fate aside, his words have become well-worn over the years. "There but for the grace of God go I" ranks right up there with "Things could always be worse." Or telling a child at the dinner table, "Clean your plate because there are starving children in Africa." It's important for all of us to realize how good we have it, and comparing our situation to someone else's is usually part and parcel of the realization.

At the same time, like #blessed, "There but for the grace of God go I" doesn't quite sit well with me. How does the following sit with you? "I'm thankful that I'm not destitute, or in jail, or in a job I hate. There but for the grace of God go I. I'm thankful that I had loving parents, a stable childhood, and the ability to pursue my dreams, especially when I know that much of the world isn't set up with those opportunities. There but for the grace of God go I. I'm thankful for my health and the use of all my faculties, that I'm not in a wheelchair or, worse, a mental institution. There but for the grace of God go I."

What's wrong here? For one, "There but for the grace of God go I" can ignore a variety of systems that bestow advantage, like race and class privilege. Or, worse, it can attribute those systems to God's grace. This saying can also create a sense of stratification on a spiritual level, as if I'm the recipient of God's grace or blessing, while the person I'm comparing myself to is not. And there's the trap that lies in comparison. As others have pointed out before me, as soon as we draw a line between ourselves and someone else, we're likely to find that God's grace is on the other side of that line—whether the line is between the haves and the have-nots, the righteous and the sinful, or the healthy and the sick.

But what if the comparison is contained within your own experience? We all grow and change, ideally for the better, which means we can look back and thank God for how far we've come. I once had someone stop to pray with me, and she ended up singing "Amazing Grace" at the top of her lungs right there on the sidewalk. It was truly spectacular—not spectacular as far as the singing went (quite the opposite, in fact) but a spectacular public witness to the power of God's deliverance. In her case, this meant deliverance from a drug addiction that had brought her to the brink of death. And where had she found God's grace? In her darkest hour.

I don't have an answer to the comparison trap that can creep into counting our blessings, nor do I think it matters all that much the specific words we use when talking about God's grace in our lives. "There but for the grace of God go I" is perfectly fine if our hearts are in the right place and we're not looking down on anybody. All the better if it leads us to compassion and good works.

The thing to remember is that God's grace and truly abundant love rain down on everyone. We can thank God until we're blue in the face, but if we don't recognize our need for these things, then we're missing out. We're effectively putting up umbrellas. We're shielding ourselves from the fullness of blessing that God intends for our lives. I think of the cancer survivor and the woman singing "Amazing Grace." Perhaps the best variation on John Bradford's words is "Here by the grace of God go I."

Here's a fair question: How do we close the umbrella that shields us from grace? How do we remove the barrier and begin to feel our need for God, especially if our lives look like one big #blessed social media post?

Take this guy, for example, who stopped by one Tuesday morning. Sleek haircut. Sharp suit. Expensive watch. Late thirties or early forties. Very rarely does a man fitting this description stop to talk to me. I'm not entirely sure why, but I have an idea. Asking for a blessing, especially in public, is an admission of need or at least of wanting something more. For some people, prayer belies the picture-perfect image of having it all together. Not to mention the belief that we can live up to the image.

So I was surprised when this man didn't just admit need. He admitted guilt: "I love my wife and kids, but sometimes they feel like a burden." He didn't mean a financial burden but a burden on his time. His work was challenging and fulfilling and required a lot of his attention. I knew the sentiment exactly, although I had never been brave enough to put it in those words. Who wants to call their family a burden? Yet there are only twenty-four hours in a day, and the demands of our professional lives and personal lives often add up to more.

When my daughter was nearing three years old, I remember my heart sinking because I realized her upcoming birthday party felt like just another item on my to-do list. And I don't mean preparations for the party, which I'd have to somehow fit into an already overflowing schedule; I mean the party itself. I thought I should be looking forward to this celebration of her life or at least not putting it in same category as a trip to the grocery store. But no such luck.

I can't remember now if I enjoyed the party or the planning. But it's okay if I didn't because I know she did. And way more often than not, I enjoy *her*. It's okay to feel that loved ones are a burden every now and again. God knows my daughter, now nearly a teenager, feels that way about me. As I told the young father, the point is to treat them like the blessings they are. In his case, this meant giving his family his full, undivided attention with what precious time he had. It also meant asking for God's grace to accomplish just that. God is here to help us with every little thing at every single turn, including resisting the temptation to check work email during dinner.

This is the beauty of prayer. The more we seek God's grace, the more we realize we need it and the better we're able to receive it. Engaging this cycle over time results in a deeper dependence on God and living out the paradoxical truth that "whenever I am weak, then I am strong."

Does this mean life gets easier when we're dependent on God? Not exactly. When my daughter was four years old, our house was just a couple of blocks from her pre-school. After picking her up one day, she told me on the walk home, "Mama, I'll carry my backpack, and you carry me." Funny how she thought that if *she* carried her backpack, it would lighten my load. Yet it was understandable since she still felt the backpack's weight when I picked her up.

God is the one who carries us while we carry our backpacks. God doesn't wear the backpack for us, removing hardship or erasing workload. But God helps us carry those things because God carries us. Christ's yoke is easy, and his burden is light, as Matthew 11:30 reminds us, no matter how many children with backpacks are in his arms.

To put it another way, "Things still suck, but prayer helps." This came from one of the more candid people I've encountered in my ministry. The first time she stopped for a blessing, I asked what she wanted me to pray for. "Oh, you know, misery." She said it so nonchalantly. There was a touch of humor in her voice, and she gave me a wry smile. But I could tell she was dead serious. Misery. Her misery.

She didn't want to talk specifics, so I launched into a prayer. Unfortunately, I botched it at the end—or so I thought. On the whole, the prayer was fine, but I closed with something about asking God to grant her a "spirit of gratitude." Of course, by now it's clear that I consider having an "attitude of gratitude" a perfectly wonderful and incredibly important spiritual practice. Indeed, we cannot live a Christian life without it. Yet I'm not out on the sidewalk to offer unsolicited spiritual advice, especially as part of a prayer. As the woman walked away, I realized how preachy I might have sounded. I've heard plenty of ministers package little sermons into prayers during church, and I wondered if that's what I'd just done.

Fortunately, this woman didn't seem too bothered by it because she returned the next week. I came to find out she had turned her back on the church years ago. But after our initial encounter, she started praying again. Then after a couple of months, she told her college-aged children about how she had started praying. She said she regretted that she hadn't raised them in the Christian tradition but was eager to let them know the power of prayer in her life now. She wanted to let them know that "things still suck, but prayer helps." And guess what? She said it all started with cultivating a spirit of gratitude. It all started with counting her blessings. Praise God, from whom all blessings flow.

If we want to get all textbook about it (or Episcopal prayer book about it, to be more specific), praising God isn't exactly the same thing as thanking God. Thanksgiving is about recognizing what God has done in the world and in our lives. Praise is about articulating who God is and what God is like, something we do by singing hymns, for example. But the two obviously overlap. Naming God's blessings with gratitude and humility (thanksgiving) naturally leads us to praise. Conversely, naming God as loving and good (praise) leads us to give thanks in all circumstances.

I grew up hearing and offering "praise reports" in my various pockets of evangelical Christian community. Any form of good news was a praise report—a reason for praising God and a cause for rejoicing. A successful surgery with no complications, landing a new job, and good weather on someone's wedding day would all be considered praise reports. Some might scoff at the simplistic sound of that, hearing a ring of pat theology or vapid faith. But I continue to use this terminology in my ministry because it helps people recognize God at work in their lives. When asked, most people of faith can come up with a praise report, even if it's along the lines of "things still suck, but prayer helps."

>>>>>>>>>>>>>

Fortunately, I'm privy to frequent praise reports in this ministry. I once heard three in rapid-fire succession. First, a woman I'd seen two months prior came barreling down the sidewalk with a to-go cup in each hand. She handed me an almond latte with turmeric as an odd but delicious thank-you, explaining that the prayer I'd offered for her several weeks ago had worked. She was less fearful and more confident. Then she asked me to pray for her ailing parents. But on my own time, please. She had to get to a meeting.

Next, a man told me he'd just gotten an MRI. While he would normally need to take a Valium in order to handle the feeling of being in such a confined space as an MRI machine, this time he got through the experience by relying on the Serenity Prayer. So we prayed it together right then and there: "God, grant me the serenity to accept the things I cannot change, courage to change the things I can, and wisdom to know the difference."

Then another woman told me she had recently prayed and fasted for two days straight for her son to "stop smoking weed." God took the desire for marijuana away from him, gave him mental clarity, and removed the fog of depression. She had walked around the block three times while I was talking to other people, waiting to share her amazing news and testimony with me.

Her story reminded me of my own experience giving up cigarettes in college. It happened after winter recess of my senior year. As soon as I came back for spring semester, I tried to take a smoke break outside the library, but inhaling burned my lungs. *Weird*, I thought. I lit up a cigarette at a party that weekend and thought it tasted disgusting. I tried again after another drink, and the result was the same. I had had absolutely no desire to give up this little vice. But there I was, wanting to enjoy something that was, simply put, no longer enjoyable. I was disappointed at first, but it didn't take long to realize this was a gift from God. All of a sudden, I had a praise report that I shouted from the rooftops. Cue the eye rolls from my friends.

What I find most striking about the praise reports I hear in this ministry is the passion and true glee with which they are told. On the day I received three in a row, I'd barely said a word before each person spilled their good news. It was like me telling my college friends how God "cured" me of smoking.

The excitement is telling. It seems that in counting blessings, the people I meet are not that focused on taking stock of what they've amassed or accomplished. Rather, they pay more attention to the ways that God shows up for them, from memorable life events to small everyday graces.

And here's the thing: when our eyes are attuned to look for those graces, they will always bubble up. One of my Tuesday regulars told me that after receiving her first blessing, she'd started seeing a "string of sacredness" all around her. I knew exactly what she was talking about, and I loved the way she put words to that sudden gift of sight that prayer can bestow. Here are a few comparisons. Right now, my knee is hurt, and I've started noticing all kinds of people wearing knee braces. When I was pregnant, it seems that I passed at least twenty pregnant women on the sidewalk in any given day. Similarly, my mother-in-law says she keeps seeing old people (although, for the record, I don't consider her old).

Point being: when we're sensitive or attuned to a certain reality, we're more likely to see it all around us. Perhaps you've heard the saying "If you look for good in the world, you'll find it. If you look for evil in the world, you'll find it." It only makes sense that if you look for the divine in the world, you'll find that too. I think this is why so many people say they feel spiritual when they are out in nature. In the great outdoors, we don't have to look very hard before we're smacked in the face by the beautiful handiwork of our Creator.

One summer, I ran vacation Bible school for the children in my church. We had a long string of what looked like Christmas lights with big colored bulbs. Every time a child identified a "God sighting" from the day before, they got to screw in a bulb and make it light up. According to the kids, God showed up in flowers, blowing bubbles, hugs from Mom and Dad, and several ways the kids were kind to one another. They were on the lookout for God.

Another way to think about God sightings is *Merriam-Webster*'s definition of a miracle: "an extraordinary event manifesting divine intervention in human affairs." The "extraordinary event" part of that definition arguably confines miracles to things that have no explanation apart from the supernatural: the parting of the Red Sea, Peter walking on water, and Jesus's resurrection, to name a few. Then there are manifestations of divine intervention that aren't as obviously miraculous but may rise to the level of miracle nonetheless. Take David and Goliath. The fact that scrawny little David killed giant Goliath by sling-shotting a stone that hit him squarely between the eyes is not an undeniable act of God. It could have happened without divine intervention. But most likely God was all over it, especially in giving David the chutzpah to stand up against a giant.

If we want to get more contemporary with our examples of the miraculous, consider these scenarios. Figuring out how to solve an urgent problem after praying for guidance. Meeting your future spouse and somehow knowing that you're meant to be together. A nudge in your thinking to call a friend, only to discover that friend is in desperate need of your emotional support. A physical sensation or vision you receive while in prayer. A voice in your head or piercing thought that seems to come out of nowhere. The overnight loss of the ability to enjoy a cigarette.

The core of Christianity—of any religious faith, really—always remains miraculous. Yet Christian thought suggests we are meant to cooperate with God so much that divine intervention doesn't *feel* all that miraculous. Instead, it feels normal, expected. God is going to show up for you. We have to be careful not to create expectations of *how* God is going to show up. But we can trust that Jesus wants to be there for us, will be there for us, and will make himself known to us, actually intervening in the world on our behalf.

There is a scientific principle that changing one thing can change everything. It's sometimes called *the butterfly effect*, which has nothing to do with actual butterflies, by the way, but with what the principle looks like when graphed. It resembles the *shape* of a butterfly. The point is that tiny changes in big systems can have complex results. By shifting one element of the pattern, the entire pattern must change. Our primary place of agency is ourselves, so we can apply the butterfly effect to our lives. Think of one thing—one way that you can make yourself more available to God. Maybe you want to talk to God over your morning cup of coffee, turning those inner thoughts that we all have into a sacred conversation. Or read a daily devotional. Or offer up a prayer when you learn about a tragedy in the news. Or practice routine kindness toward people you find difficult.

Just make that one intentional change. See if it disrupts your pattern. My bet is that God will seize the opportunity to break in with miraculous grace. And then do you know what happens? Today's miraculous can become tomorrow's normal. What is shocking now becomes understood in the realm of faith. And what seems impossible will become possible with God.

4

SPIRITUAL SUPERPOWERS

What's so special about a blessing from a priest? Are my prayers more effective because I'm clergy? Does it have anything to do with how I live my life or just the office I hold? Maybe I should have asked my first kneeler— as in, a person who kneeled down to receive a blessing. Kneeling is an act of piety that many people do in church. But on the concrete? Not so much.

Even more surprising than watching someone kneel down in front of me on the sidewalk was that this person spoke with his mouth full. He had a Diet Coke in one hand and a breakfast sandwich in the other. Before

I had a chance to acknowledge his request, he closed his eyes and stopped chewing. This was his signal that he was ready to be blessed. And I quickly realized that I had better get the show on the road.

I didn't ask for a prayer request in this instance as he was clearly moving right to the blessing part. Rather, I went straight for a quick riff on a standard blessing: "The blessing of God Almighty, Father, Son, and Holy Spirit, be upon you, shine through you, and make you a blessing to all those you encounter today." The man stood up while nodding his thanks, took another bite of his sandwich, and hurried along his way. The whole thing literally took less than ten seconds.

I had a similar speedy experience when a man came up to me while talking on his cell phone. He was using earbuds and said, "*Un segundo*" as he pulled one from his ear and let it drop. He remained on the call with one ear while being able to listen to me with the other. I was amused. He had put his conversation partner on hold so he could ask for a blessing. After our brief interaction, he popped the dangling earbud back into his ear and picked right back up with his call. He'd assumed that receiving a blessing would only take one second, and he was right. It only takes a second to form a connection with someone. It only takes a second to shut out the rest of the world and give God a moment of our undivided attention. It only takes a second to remember that the Holy Spirit is all around us, closer than a whisper.

Is that what these people were after—human connection, focus on God, and the felt presence of the Holy Spirit? Yeah, I think they were, even though they rolled through our encounter like they were ordering blessings at a drive-through window.

Here's an additional possibility. When I told a clergy friend about the guy who kneeled for a blessing while eating on the go, he said, "Blessing is recognizing the good in someone. It's where our ministry starts, and it's what people expect, consciously or subconsciously, when they come to church."

I hope he's right. I hope the man with the breakfast sandwich, the man with the earbuds, and all the people who stop to talk to me on the sidewalk know, on some level, that God is looking to honor and affirm the good in us. God is looking to tell us we are loved so that we can love ourselves enough to live with integrity. This desire of God's heart is a reason we can "approach the throne of grace with boldness," asking for whatever we need and whatever gifts God has for us.

At the end of every Sunday service, I pronounce a blessing over the people gathered. I'm usually standing in front of our high altar—seventy-five feet from the congregation and high enough to look out over everyone. Blessing a congregation is very similar to blessing an individual except that I don't touch anyone's forehead. Instead, I make the sign of the cross in a giant sweeping motion with my hand while saying the same words: "The blessing of God Almighty, the Father, the Son, and the Holy Spirit, be among you and remain with you always." Then we all say together, "Amen."

The corresponding movement from congregation members is to cross themselves while I'm blessing them. To cross yourself, you use the fingers of your right hand to touch your forehead (at the word *Father*), then heart or upper abdomen (*Son*), left shoulder (*Holy*), right shoulder (*Spirit*), and, optionally, your heart again (*Amen*). Crossing oneself is an ancient Christian gesture, perhaps as old as the fourth century. When done in worship, it marks our engagement of head, heart, body, and soul at various times throughout the service. In my church, some people cross themselves at the mention of God's promise of resurrection during certain prayers. Some also cross themselves before receiving the Eucharist. In this case, the gesture becomes a prayer in itself—a prayer for God to purify their hearts in preparation to receive the body and blood of Christ. Most congregants cross themselves at two key moments, mirroring me as I make the sign of the cross over the congregation. The first is when I declare God's forgiveness of sin. The second is during the final blessing.

Standing on the sidewalk, I've had this sort of "cross exchange" with people who wave at me from the other side of the street or bus drivers who honk to get my attention. I bless them from a distance, and they cross themselves in response. One driver even brought his bus to a complete stop in front of me, opened his door for a blessing, and then drove away after receiving one.

What's all this crossing about? The Christian faith tells us the cross is a demonstration of God's sacrificial love. It's a means of forgiveness, an instrument of reconciliation between us and God. It's a paradox of death conquering death, a subversion of worldly power, and an embodiment of a new energy let loose in the world. I admit that when I cross myself, I often go through the motions without thinking about any of these things. But when I bring intention to the movement, I consciously call on the love of Jesus. I claim the power of the cross to make me a new creation because "I have been crucified with Christ; and it is no longer I who live, but it is Christ who lives in me."

There are other aspects of the cross to claim as well. Forgiveness. Fearlessness. The possibility of another way to live. God's solidarity in our suffering. What does Jesus's death on a cross represent for you? What does a dying God offer? Think of what you need to call unto yourself and receive into your soul. Consider asking for it now in the name of God, Father, Son, and Holy Spirit. Amen.

〉〉〉〉〉〉〉〉〉〉

In addition to blessing people, the church has a long tradition of blessing places, objects, occasions, and, of course, animals. St. Francis of Assisi is the patron saint of animals, and many Christian denominations celebrate St. Francis Day, October 4, with the blessing of animals either in church or outdoors.

During my years of ministry, I've blessed lots of dogs, plenty of cats, guinea pigs, birds, and even a snake. Add to that stuffed animals and pictures of pets who are deceased. I'm not sure what I believe about the souls of departed pets, but I've seen enough grieving pet owners not to care. If blessing a picture will bring a little comfort, give me that pic.

It's no surprise that people can be extremely invested in their pets, especially if they have a pet who is their primary companion. As a cat lover told me, "They just crawl into your heart." One woman who brought her dog to be blessed said that God had miraculously woken her up at 2:00 a.m. so she could save her dog's life. She found the dog in the kitchen with his entire head stuck inside his treat jar, which would have suffocated him had she not been there. Another woman told me how her dog saved *her* life by showing loyalty, love, and affection during a dark time. The dog gave her a reason to live, which was to care and provide for him. For a time, that was enough. No wonder these women showed up for Blessing of the Animals.

Several years ago, I did a Blessing of the Animals service in Central Park with my good friend Ryan, a former clergy colleague. It was a bright and beautiful Sunday afternoon in October, and we were celebrating St. Francis Day. We had walked over from our church to the park after morning services and gathered with thirty or so people and twenty or so animals (mainly dogs) in a large circle in a grassy area. We sang and prayed, and Ryan and I blessed some quite vocal and squirmy pets.

An onlooker thought we were conducting a dog wedding when he first walked up. I found this out years later when I came across a blog post he wrote about attending this Blessing of the Animals service. The post included video footage of Ryan's sermon, in which he quoted a late liturgical scholar, Thomas Talley: "To bless something is to say something nice to God about it." This isn't the only way to define *blessing*, but it's one to remember. And it's right in line with the idea articulated by my other friend who commented on my blessing of the man with the breakfast sandwich—that blessing is recognizing the good in someone.

Affirming goodness is an important part of my ministry. Frankly, it's something I try to do in all realms of life, from parenting to pastoring to conversations with friends and family. I'm even working on affirming the goodness in myself, as hard as that can sometimes be. I may forever be my own worst critic, but seeing the good in others reminds me there's good in me too.

In all these attempts to affirm goodness, in others in and in myself, this verse of Scripture is a big help: "Finally, beloved, whatever is true, whatever is honorable, whatever is just, whatever is pure, whatever is pleasing, whatever is commendable, if there is any excellence and if there is anything worthy of praise, think about these things."

Was the author writing about praising a three-year-old for sharing? Or thanking a member of the military for their service? Or giving yourself permission to bask in the glow of a recent accomplishment? Probably not, but the lesson still applies. Our goodness comes from God, so it's naturally something to contemplate in its many forms and then celebrate and affirm in one another. In the context of blessing, these words of affirmation hold great power. They certainly did for the man who blogged about Blessing of the Animals:

> And though I am in no way religious, this ceremony to bless our beloved pets reaffirmed my faith in humanity somehow. A cursory glance at the internet and you'll see a cascade of dead bodies, infectious microbes, and civil unrest. All the crazy shit going on everywhere. And then this, somebody took the time to do a nice thing, a small thing true, lacking the fire of political revolution or the potential downfall of humanity in an airborne plague, but no less important. Two Anglican priests blessed dogs (and all other creatures) in Central Park on a beautiful early fall day. And then, almost as quickly as it had begun it was over. What was the meaning of it all, I wondered? What was the takeaway?

He closed his post with a prayer attributed to St. Francis: "Where there is hatred, let us sow love; where there is injury, pardon; where there is discord, union; where there is despair, hope; where there is darkness, light; where there is sadness, joy. Grant that we may not so much seek to be consoled as to console; to be understood as to understand; to be loved as to love. For it is in giving that we receive; it is in pardoning that we are free."

》》》》》》》》》》》

One of my regulars for a sidewalk blessing is a man so spiritual that he seems to exist on a higher plane. There's something very calming about his presence. He speaks quietly but with joy. His face is peaceful and relaxed. And the light of God seems to shine through his eyes. When I first met him, he asked for a simple prayer: that God would use him. He has a palpable openness and willingness to be led by the Holy Spirit through life. We often talk about our shared desire to be vessels of grace and what a privilege it is to share God's love when the opportunity arises. During the COVID-19 pandemic, *New York Eyewitness News* did a story on my "Ask me for a blessing" ministry. The point was to feature how our church was reaching people even when our building was closed. On the Tuesday that a reporter and camera crew came by to film, my friend on a higher plane happened to be walking by and happily agreed to be interviewed. He relished the opportunity to speak about God on TV, as did I.

After the news segment aired, he seemed even more excited about sharing his faith. One day, he asked me to come bless his doorman. "Great idea," I said. It's kind of like inviting a friend to church is a great idea. In this case, however, we were bringing church to a friend. Of course, I should have asked him why he thought of it in the first place. Was his doorman particularly faithful? Or perhaps going through a tough time? Too bad I let that opportunity slip by, but fortunately I had something else in mind.

I left my post in front of the church, and we walked over to his apartment building, which was less than a block away. The doorman gave me a wide-eyed look, clearly caught off guard, mostly likely because of my vestments. But after a few words of introduction, he seemed to relax. I still didn't know why my friend had asked me to come and bless his doorman, but I was excited to affirm some goodness. I told him that I'd recently asked the teens in my church's high-school youth group to name the five most important people in their lives. Each one included their doorman, who had been a constant over the years and ultimately served a role in their upbringing.

I had been surprised to hear this from the high schoolers at first, but then I thought, *How true!* My family lived in a building with a doorman for just two years, yet it was long enough for my daughter to come home excited to see Mr. Eddie every day after kindergarten and first grade. We even went back to visit him—multiple times—after we moved away.

The doorman standing in front of me heard the truth these high schoolers had lifted up. It was good, life-affirming news to him indeed. He gladly received a blessing for his ministry of hospitality, especially as offered to children. Perhaps he too had a desire that God would use him.

Along the lines of recognizing the good in someone is recognizing, simply, their worth. I once had a woman come up and stand silently before me on the sidewalk. Her facial expression was hard to make out because she was wearing giant sunglasses. I asked if she'd like a blessing, and she nodded. I asked if there was anything in particular that she needed prayer for. She was silent for a moment and then she choked out, "Me." Her chin trembled, and a tear ran down her cheek. This woman needed to be assured of her worth in God's eyes. I prayed that in that moment, she would know God's unconditional, unwavering, deep, abiding love for her; that she would feel that love bursting forth from her heart and traveling to the tips of her fingers and toes; and that she would rest in the assurance of her infinite value as God's very own beloved child. Amen.

Christianity affirms our belovedness. It affirms the wideness of God's love, mercy, and grace. But it has mixed messages around worth. I'm reminded of this every year during the season of Lent. As mentioned earlier, Lent is a penitential season, one focused on coming to terms with human frailty and sin. Consequently, some churches, mine included, will add the Prayer of Humble Access before receiving Communion. This prayer begins with the line "We are not worthy so much as to gather up the crumbs from under Thy table."

A few people have told me they hate the Prayer of Humble Access because of that line. One woman said it makes her wince. I understand her reaction. If we're not worthy to gather crumbs under God's table, does this mean we're not worthy to receive the bread and the wine? Are we not worthy to be God's children? Are we not worthy of God's love?

Some Christians would say, "No, we are *not* worthy of God's love. We are so sinful, and God is so holy, that God can't even be near us but for the fact that Jesus died. Jesus stands between us and the Father so that when the Father looks at us, he sees Jesus's righteousness rather than our sin. That's what protects us from his wrath." This is what I was taught as a child.

I don't buy this argument now. I don't believe Jesus needs to protect us from God the Father—God the Creator, who calls us good, in whose image we are made, whose law is written on our hearts, and who loves us like a mama bear fiercely protecting her cubs. Why would we need protection from the One protecting us?

At the same time, I think the Prayer of Humble Access is trying to get at the point that we don't deserve God's grace in the sense that grace is, by definition, unmerited. It can't be earned and, conversely, can't be taken away. This means we don't approach the altar with a sense of entitlement, but with reverence, humility, and gratitude.

Yet I think there's a distinction that the Prayer of Humble Access misses. Can we be worthy of grace without deserving it? Yes, we can. The only people who can benefit from God's saving grace are sinners. To say we have to be perfect—or without sin—in order to be saved from our sins is a logical disconnect. A perfect person doesn't need salvation. Jesus didn't need salvation. *We* do. Otherwise, salvation wouldn't exist. Its mere existence means that we are worth redeeming. Jesus died on the cross because it was worth it. We are worth it. You are worth it. And Jesus wants us to receive the fullness of the salvation that flows from his death and resurrection. He wants us to experience the fullness of life in Christ.

When I bless someone, I am essentially saying, "You are worth it. And the cross I make on your forehead is a sign of that worth, which cannot be removed. Even when your behavior is not worthy of a loving response, even when it causes God pain, Christ's love as demonstrated on the cross remains because of your infinite worth to him."

It's a message worthy of internalizing. But is it one you have to be ordained to pronounce? Is there something magical or sacred or super-spiritual about a clergyperson being the one to offer a blessing?

》》》》》》》》》》》》

In my Christian denomination, only a priest can bless and consecrate. Only a priest can bless a person—or anything, for that matter—and only a priest can consecrate the bread and the wine in the Eucharist so that it becomes infused with the presence of Jesus. This is an important tenet of faith for Episcopalians, but I've got to be honest: I'm not completely sold on it.

I know that my church has designated me to bless and consecrate as an Episcopal priest, and I respect the office that I hold. I'm not looking to change church doctrine, nor would I expect my congregation to accept anything different. Yet I wonder if our views are a little narrow on this point, especially when it comes to blessing. Would my blessings be any less efficacious if I were a layperson?

Sometimes I think not. Just as God's grace is available to all, I believe the ability to *impart* that grace can belong to anyone, regardless of ordination status or even belief system. But once, when I was almost convinced that ordination doesn't make that much of a difference, a friend who is also an Episcopal bishop stopped for a chat and a blessing from me. As he walked away, he looked back at me, held up a hand, and said the words "Easter blessings!"

I know it sounds strange, but it was as if a superpower shot from his hand and hit me in the heart. A tingly heat radiated through my chest and quickly dissipated. It was gone as quickly as it had come, and I felt blessed at a visceral level.

Part of the issue, and my struggle, is my Christian tradition's understanding of what happens in ordination. Priests are ordained by bishops in a special service that involves taking certain vows to study Scripture, remain persistent in prayer, perform the sacraments, be a faithful pastor, and pattern our lives after the teachings of Jesus. Then a bishop lays hands on your head in the act of making you a priest. Some say that at this moment there is an ontological change—that is, a change in the spiritual nature of one's being. I can't claim to understand this. In the moment of ordination, I know I was given a particular role in sacramental ministry. My relationship to the church changed. But a change in my *being*? I certainly didn't become holier.

Not long after my ordination, I bought a dainty necklace with a small dove set inside a flame. It was for my daughter. I was at the gift shop of Holy Cross Monastery, a community of Anglican Benedictine monks in the Hudson River Valley. As soon as I'd made my purchase, the brother at the register said enthusiastically, "Now you must bless it!"

Me? "Um, how about you bless it?" I asked him.

"Oh, I'm not a priest," he responded quickly. No, he wasn't. But he *was* a monk, with deep spiritual wisdom and kindness cultivated through decades of religious piety and devotion. I was a priest, thirty years younger, with a few months of ordained ministry under my belt. This wasn't exactly adding up in my mind, but I went with it. If he was as wise and devout as I thought him to be, I'd take his word for it.

So I made the sign of the cross over the necklace while I blessed it in the name of the Father, the Son, and the Holy Spirit. Then I let my hand hover over the necklace a moment longer. I thought a bit, and then I said something along the lines of "And may it draw forth the peace and the fire of the Holy Spirit within my daughter every time she wears it."

Nice words, right? The monk thought so, as he gave me a knowing smile and approving nod. I just wasn't too sure they did anything.

Since then, I've come to bless many more necklaces. I've blessed religious objects, such as crosses and Bibles; clothing; backpacks; and even diapers (for a diaper drive to help low-income families). I now have a stronger sense of my spiritual authority to bless, and I feel less tentative or awkward about it than I did when I blessed that necklace under a monk's insistence. Still, there's always a piece of me wondering if I'm doing anything more than stating a positive intention.

To be sure, positive intention is a form of prayer. Yet the gap between positive intention and blessing is where my doubt lies. It's a gap that faith must bridge.

Fortunately, sometimes that gap feels smaller than others, and a few times, it's shrunk down to almost nothing.

One of those times was when a friend asked me to bless a set of rosary beads left to her by her late grandmother. She had stored them away and recently uncovered them while doing some spring cleaning. The usual doubts I have around blessing objects arose within me. But I said, "Sure," and held out my hand.

She dropped the beads into my palm, and I placed my other hand on top so that they were in a loose clasp. The string of beads felt light and cool. They were nothing fancy, but I could feel an energy radiating off of them—energy that I knew must have come from the prayers of her grandmother as she moved her fingers along the beads.

It reminded me of the feeling I get when I walk into a sacred space that seems to be charged by the presence and prayers of worshippers before me. The chapel at New York-Presbyterian Hospital always feels that way to me. Every time I visit a patient there, I go into that chapel, where I know people of all religions have poured out their hearts to God, pleading and often in pain.

It's as if their faith has seeped into the walls, and I like to believe that my own prayers and practice of the presence of God do too.

When I held those rosary beads, I simply added to the spiritual energy that was already there. The blessing began like a light emanating from my heart chakra, traveling down my arms and through my hands, more important than any words I could muster. Of course, I did muster some words of blessing, mainly on account of my friend, who was watching me closely. Blessing an object is about blessing the person who receives that object. It's about asking God to make it a tangible means of grace for the benefit of the owner.

This is somewhat similar to what happens with the water in baptism and the bread and wine in the Eucharist. The power of the Holy Spirit meets the prayerful intention of the pastor or priest. The result is a tangible means of grace. The result is blessing.

I will probably always wonder about the "power" to bless that was conferred upon me by ordination. Was it power from God? The church? Both? I know that clergy who become enamored of such power, and their special call to wield it, sometimes end up doing great harm to themselves and their flock. Yet I also know that when I was ordained, the prayerful intention of my bishop was met by the power of the Holy Spirit. I felt it when he placed his hands on my head and prayed, "Father, through Jesus Christ your Son, give your Holy Spirit to Adrian; fill her with grace and power, and make her a priest in your Church." The tingling I've come to associate with the Holy Spirit radiated through my body. I wept, for this act of ordination met my prayerful intention too.

Was there really an ontological change? Maybe. For me, the answer doesn't matter all that much. Regardless of what I'm blessing—person, animal, liquid, solid—I bring prayerful intention to spoken word and shine light energy forth from my heart. The rest is up to God.

>>>>>>>>>>>>

When I think about light energy, I always remember an experience I had as a hospital chaplain sitting with a patient in the emergency room. I don't remember what brought him in, but I do remember praying for him. Then he offered to pray for me. He took my hand and held it in both of his, my elbow resting on the hospital bed. He prayed in Spanish, too quickly for me to keep up with any hope of translating. But I was too distracted by the tingling sensation in my arm to pay much attention to words anyway. This man was not ordained in any Christian denomination. Yet the Holy Spirit certainly flowed through him. And if I saw him today, I'd definitely ask him for a blessing.

Ordained or not, you have light energy too. It comes from the divine spark within each of us. If you've never intentionally used your light to bless other people, here's a suggestion for how to start. Ever heard of the Care Bear stare? If you're a child of the 1980s and early '90s, then maybe so. The Care Bears shine light from their tummy symbols on a given individual, and it has a healing effect on that person. The light of Christ in us can function in a similar way.

If you want to bless someone, whether in your mind or in person, blast them with the light and love of Christ. If you're in a position to touch the person, let the light travel through your hand. Otherwise, I'd say shine it from your heart rather than your tummy but, hey, your call. Do it for those you like and also those you don't.

Jesus said to "bless those who curse you," after all. And the next time you try it on someone you dislike, I guarantee it will have a healing effect—most likely on you.

Finally, be liberal in offering your blessings. I love it when someone pauses to read my "Ask me for a blessing" sign and responds by saying, "God bless *you!*" (The one exception was a man who said it as he creepily looked me up and down. You better believe he got an earful.)

The strangest blessing I've received came from a woman walking up the sidewalk while talking on her cell phone. When she got near me, she slowed her pace just long enough to bless me. She took the phone away from her ear, drew a cross through the air with it, and mouthed the words "God bless you." Then she kept moving, never missing a beat in her conversation.

It was one of the more hilarious moments in my ministry, right up there with the guy who kneeled for a blessing while having breakfast on the go. Not only was it funny, but there was also something I could appreciate about the blending of the sacred with the secular. The juxtaposition of the woman's cell phone with making the sign of the cross was like the juxtaposition of the man's breakfast sandwich with his formal posture of kneeling.

I loved the casualness of it all. God is involved in the details of our lives, right down to the minutiae, and is ready to meet us at every turn. We can invite God into whatever we're doing, whether it's washing the dishes or walking to work. We can pray anytime, anywhere. Why can't the same hold true for blessings? Receiving a blessing is a way of publicly acknowledging that we want God in our lives. A priest's blessing may be imparted with the weight of the church, but anyone's blessing can be imparted with the weight of the Holy Spirit, even if mediated through a cell phone.

This world needs more blessing, not just from clergy but from all people of God. Blessings filled with humor, compassion, encouragement, hope. Blessings born of gratitude, forgiveness, empathy, and, of course, love. Just as the Holy Spirit hovered over the waters of the earth at the beginning of creation, the Spirit hovers over our world today, waiting to unleash her power. Waiting to meet our prayerful intentions with spiritual energy. Waiting to bless through you.

5

I DIDN'T ASK FOR THAT BLESSING

When I told a friend that I was writing this book, I described the overall project as unpacking the word *blessing*. She let out a long "Ooooooo." There was a look of intrigue on her face and a slight smile in her eyes. I could see her mind working but wasn't sure where it was headed.

I didn't have to wait long, though. After a few seconds of silence, she mused, "Like when something really awful produces something really good."

Of course. She had lost the love of her life six months earlier. Before the conversation turned to my book, we had been talking about how much gratitude she felt for the years she and her partner had together and all the ways in which she was experiencing the nearness of his presence now. Her words were spoken through many tears and many tissues, but the undercurrent was pure love. And while the idea of something awful producing something good can be premature and even hurtful when spoken to someone who is suffering, she could authentically embrace this truth for herself.

"Exactly," I said. Sometimes blessing can be the child of sorrow, especially when it comes to grief. And I hear a lot of sorrow on the sidewalk.

"My friend died and I'm having a hard time."

"My wife just had a miscarriage."

"Today is the anniversary of my mother's passing."

Grief makes people vulnerable. In the wake of loss, we are broken, and we are broken open. This allows us to accept compassion from others more readily. For some, grief prompts them to seek spiritual comfort in organized religion. It's no surprise, then, when someone who stops for a blessing ends up telling me about the loss of a loved one, often with a shaky voice and teary eyes. We pray, we lament, we name the sting of death for those left behind, even if death has no sting for those now in heaven.

A clergy colleague once told me she lost her son to suicide when he was a teenager. It had been many years since his death, and she explained her experience of loss, grief, and resurrection in terms similar to these: When we go through the death of a loved one, our hearts are stretched. Our hearts need more room to accommodate the pain of loss. The answer is not for the pain to displace other things in our hearts, like faith or hope. The answer is for our hearts to grow bigger. Then when the pain lessens, bit by bit, the space it occupied remains. The heart has increased capacity and can be filled with other things—more peace, more joy, more love, more fruit of the Holy Spirit.

This has been my experience with many types of loss—loss of a dream, loss of a relationship, loss of an overly simplistic understanding of God, and, yes, loss of a loved one. When the depths of our pain meet the depths of God's unwavering love, we may cry tears of grief and gratitude and joy and sorrow all mixed together.

And we can receive even more of God's love poured into our hearts.

Yet getting to this place of blessing through the path of pain can be a difficult journey.

》》》》》》》》》》

"My wife's father was murdered a year ago, and her emotions still erupt like a volcano."

I've heard a lot of surprising things in this ministry, but for some reason, this one really took me aback. Perhaps it was the apt metaphor the man used—a volcano—to describe grief in the wake of a murder. Or perhaps it was the look of utter helplessness on the man's face, with a little exhaustion mixed in. Supporting a loved one through traumatic loss is hard work, and he'd been at it for a year.

It wasn't very long ago that a year was the official time period for mourning. Family members of the departed wore all black. They didn't go to parties or smile very much, and everybody accepted this as normal. Yet here was this husband a year after his father-in-law's death, and he hadn't seen much movement in his wife's grief process. "She's stuck in the anger stage," he said.

He was referring to the stages of grief from death-and-dying expert Elisabeth Kübler-Ross: denial, anger, bargaining, depression, and acceptance. *Stages* is a bit of a misnomer because they aren't exactly linear. As a country pastor explained to me years ago, the stages of grief are like different types of wild animals that can show up on your porch at nighttime: you never know which one is going to appear. Or for how long it will keep coming. The process of grief is very personal, and each person is entitled to their own schedule.

While I don't have much experience with grief and homicide, I do know about anger in dealing with loss, especially anger at God in the face of injustice. Anger of the "it's not fair" variety. Grief can leave us feeling out of control, and people of faith usually see God as ultimately *in* control. It makes sense that we might look to the One in charge when things go wrong and take our complaints to the top.

This may result in laying into God with accusations or giving God the cold shoulder for a while. The good news is that anger at God can be a sign of our intimacy with God, even if it doesn't feel that way in the moment. Over time, that intimacy pulls us back in. Love pulls us back into relationship and heals the rift. This may include forgiving God for letting us down or acknowledging that we're tired of holding a grudge.

Do we as humans actually forgive God? I admit that is a radical concept. I remember reading the following poem in my late twenties and being totally scandalized:

> With all humility
> I say,
>
> it is God who should ask forgiveness,
> not we, Him.
>
> Someday you will know this.
> A saint could
> explain.

These words come from St. John of the Cross, a sixteenth-century Spanish monk and mystical poet who suffered greatly for his faith. I knew John had endured terrible treatment at the hands of the church and that he was a lot closer to God than I would likely ever be.

But to say God needs forgiveness from *us*? What kind of heresy is that?

Ten years later, I heard this concept again, this time from a Catholic sister who suggested I consider forgiving God for essentially not performing a miracle in my life. I had been through the agony of secondary infertility—not being able to carry a baby to term after already having a child. After years of miscarriage, expensive and painful fertility treatments, and strain on my marriage, I was despondent. And pissed. I truly thought God wanted me to have a baby and that God would make a way. Eventually, I concluded that I must have been wrong or God changed God's mind for some reason unbeknownst to me.

Either way, I knew God didn't owe me a miracle. We believe in miracles, but we don't rely on them. So what was this business about forgiving God for not granting me a miracle?

Like many Christians, I thought that if I felt neglected by God or disappointed in God or mad at God, my job was to move beyond it. That's how I understood the book of Job. Job has all kinds of terrible things happen to him and eventually asks God, "What gives?" God basically says in response, "I don't owe you any explanation for what's happening in your life. I created the universe, I rule the world, so who are you to challenge me?" Job is the one who ends up apologizing.

Aren't we supposed to do the same? When we get mad at God, aren't we supposed to just get over it—and then apologize to God for getting mad in the first place? I don't think so. At least not anymore.

In the Gospel of Matthew, Jesus sends a message to John the Baptist while John is in prison: "Go tell John what you hear and see. The blind receive sight, the lame walk, people are cured of leprosy, the deaf hear, the dead are raised, and the good news is preached to the poor. Blessed is the man who does not fall away on account of me."

Blessed is the man who does not fall away on account of me: Jesus is giving John a summation of all the miraculous things he's doing, along with an exhortation to not fall away. John is blessed if he keeps the faith. Why? Because Jesus won't be performing a miracle for him. Jesus, who has done all these wonderful things for so many others, is going to let him die by execution.

As far as we know, John did keep the faith. I imagine John went to his death willingly, with his head held high and still praising God. But I also wonder if John felt the need to forgive Jesus for not coming to his rescue.

This is one of those places where God becoming human in the person of Jesus is really helpful in thinking through questions about God. We know that human relationships benefit from free-flowing forgiveness on both sides. Since Jesus was human, perhaps this means that our relationship with him is no different.

Often, our hesitancy to forgive people is rooted in the misconception that forgiveness is only something designed to benefit the offender. In reality, forgiveness is also designed to heal the one who was wounded. When we forgive someone, we're not endorsing what happened. We're not saying we agree with it or that it was acceptable. We're just saying that we're not willing to be bitter. When we forgive, we are pronouncing that we insist on living life in freedom instead of in emotional bondage.

In light of this understanding of forgiveness, it's not even necessary that someone actually be guilty of deliberately hurting us in order for us to forgive. Often in relationships, we are hurt not because of an action that wounded us but because of a *lack* of action that disappointed us. We are hurt because other people fail to live up to our hopes and expectations of them—even when those hopes and expectations are completely unfair or unrealistic. I imagine we've all had unrealistic expectations of God and felt disappointed when God didn't meet them.

We are tempted to live with disappointment and resentment that result from our own lost hope and unfulfilled desires. In these cases, the only option that allows us to live in freedom is to forgive the person who disappointed us. Even when that person is God. I dare say *especially* when that person is God.

Perhaps you've had someone say "I forgive you" for something. And you're thinking to yourself, "I don't need your forgiveness, because I didn't do anything wrong. And it's a little bit offensive that you think I did. In fact, to *forgive* me is to *accuse* me" [incredulous gasp]!

I've been in this position, and I was offended too. But ultimately, I have to say I'm glad the person forgave me, whether I was actually at fault or not. Because otherwise they would have continued to stew over it, and there would have been a rift in our relationship. Maybe this is the posture God takes with us. Does God need to be forgiven? No. Does God welcome our forgiveness? I think God does.

Blessed are we if we keep the faith when God lets us down.

I would never encourage anyone to rush to forgiveness as a solution to anger—whether the anger is directed at God or another person. But for those feeling stuck, it can help to simply be open—open to receiving the ability to forgive as a gift of grace. A very helpful definition of forgiveness is letting go of the hope for a better past. I think God would wish that sort of letting go for all of us.

Like acceptance, which is the final stage of grief in Kübler-Ross's framework, forgiveness of something deeply hurtful is about integration of loss into our reality. It's not necessarily moving on but moving forward. Any great loss or great longing will always bring pain. Our greatest comfort will always be God. God's commitment to us is rock solid, unfailing, and everlasting.

No matter where we are in the journey of healing or the journey of faith, no matter how much we rant and rave and rage, God's love holds us fast.

)))))))))))))

God's love also holds us together when we fall apart. I once had a middle-aged man seek prayer for his daughter without telling me much about her. This is not uncommon. Not everyone wants to divulge details, especially to a stranger on the street, and prayers don't have to be peppered with personal information to be effective. Especially in this situation, it turned out.

I began to pray for this man's daughter, in general language since I didn't know specifics, and within seconds, this father was sobbing. He soon fell against my shoulder and into my arms, his body convulsing. It surprised us both. Yet his weeping also made total sense, given that this was about his child. One of the most common prayer requests I receive is that of parents seeking God's help for their children. Children who are sick or stressed, having a tough time at school or having a tough time at life. One is struggling with math. Another is struggling with meth. No matter the gradient of our children's pain or relative place on the scale of difficult things our young people face, parents feel it. Deeply.

I unlocked the church doors, led the man inside, and invited him to sit for as long as he needed. After ten minutes or so, he came back out and slipped past me with a quick nod of thanks. I can only wonder what was going on with his daughter.

I've heard that having a child is like having your heart walking around outside your body. That image is spot on in my experience. I know the feeling of heartbreak when your child is wronged or hurt or deeply disappointed. Compassion is accompanied by anger at injustice, the fierce instinct to protect, and an acute sense of helplessness because you can't fix any of it. Perhaps it's all summed up by what Simeon said to Mary. While Jesus was still a newborn, Mary and Joseph took him to the Temple to be presented to God in accordance with Jewish law. Simeon, who met Jesus and his parents as they entered the Temple, took Jesus in his arms and prophesied about his death. He told Mary, "A sword will pierce your own soul too." Some translations of the Bible use the word *heart* rather than *soul*. A sword will pierce your heart. The heart walking around outside your body.

It helps to know that Mary is the supreme example of blessedness. She calls herself blessed. Her cousin Elizabeth calls her blessed. She's known by Catholics as the Blessed Mother—and rightly so. What greater blessing is there than to be chosen as the mother of God? Yet this blessing necessarily came with burden, including watching Jesus die.

I think any parent will tell you that the loss of a child is their greatest fear, and those who have experienced such loss know it as their greatest pain. Mary knows this pain, as does God the Father. Both looked upon Jesus hanging on the cross with the suffering love of a parent.

Years ago, I tried a way of praying that was new to me: assuming the pose of a religious figure pictured in a piece of art. The idea is to model that figure's body posture and facial expression to see how it impacts your prayer experience. I chose a *pietà*: a sculpture of Mary mourning over the body of Christ after the crucifixion. It's a familiar image—Mary cradling the dead body of

Jesus in her lap—and one that's repeated thousands of times over in different churches and museums by different artists in different cultures.

After studying the image for a few days, I finally felt ready to assume Mary's posture in the *pietà*. I went so far as to drape a shawl over my head, close my eyes, and mimic her expression of grief. In my mind's eye, I turned my gaze downward, fully expecting to see Jesus. What I saw in my imagination instead was my own child, who was five years old at the time. My daughter, bruised and bloodied and dead. My eyes popped open, and I drew my hand to my mouth. I sat for a few minutes, startled and shaken.

Yet I still wanted to enter back into the vision to see what would happen. I took a deep breath and closed my eyes. But I did not see my daughter that time, nor did I see Jesus. Instead, I received a thought. Perhaps a message from God, perhaps not. But the thought was this: "Christ is all suffering, and all suffering is Christ."

Christ is all suffering. All suffering is Christ. I believe that Jesus is always with us in our suffering. He suffers alongside us because his solidarity with us is so deep. This includes ordinary suffering that simply flows from being human. It includes suffering that is inflicted unjustly by other people and systems. And it includes suffering that arises out of the struggle against injustice that is part of our call to serve God. Jesus is present wherever there is suffering.

Given the nearness of his presence, does this mean that suffering inherently involves blessing? I hesitate to say yes, at least from a place of personal experience. My lack of suffering is fantastical relative to the suffering across the world, across peoples, and across time. I'm an upper-middle-class white woman living in the United States, for heaven's sake.

But then I consider the Beatitudes. You can't write about blessing without taking on the Beatitudes, which lump affliction and blessing together. The Beatitudes appear in the Gospels of Luke and Matthew as sayings attributed to Jesus that are proverb-like blessings on people mostly considered less fortunate. When we consult the Beatitudes in both of these Gospels, we get quite the list of people whom Jesus calls blessed: the poor, the hungry, those who weep, those who mourn, the poor in spirit, the meek, the merciful, the peacemakers, the pure in heart, the persecuted, those who hunger and thirst for righteousness, and those hated and rejected because of Jesus. Why are they blessed? How does this work?

In answer to that question, Jesus points to blessings in the future. Those suffering under oppression, including Jesus's first-century listeners, will be comforted and satisfied, laugh, inherit the earth, and receive reward in heaven. A time will come when God's people will be restored and rewarded for their perseverance.

Jesus also says the kingdom of God, or the kingdom of heaven, belongs to the poor, the poor in spirit, and those who are persecuted for righteousness's sake. This implies blessing in the *present*, as opposed to the future, based on the fact that Jesus was with them. Jesus's listeners were already experiencing his presence as king. His miracles revealed what his kingdom was all about. It was a spiritual place, a way of being, and they could inhabit it then and there. Did the kingdom of God belong only to people experiencing hardship and those standing in solidarity with them? No, but the primacy Jesus gives them is undeniable.

This way of understanding the Beatitudes is consistent with liberation theology, which started as a movement in the 1960s within the Catholic Church in Latin America and also within Black churches in the United States. Liberation theology begins with the presumption that people who suffer from poverty and injustice are a privileged channel for God's grace. Because the God of the Bible is a liberator of the oppressed, and because Jesus himself was poor, oppressed, and persecuted, God is with the least and the marginal in a way that God is not with the rest of the world. God sides with them and invites everyone to do the same. Likewise, those who are impoverished are positioned to know more about God because of their poverty. They can't hope in government, money, or anything *but* God's grace. Therefore, they are more unequivocally faithful than those with options, who may have a divided heart or seek consolation in wealth rather than God. By this rationale, they are also unequivocally blessed. People with options can share in this blessedness by coming alongside those without. It is through our union with those who suffer from social, economic, and political obstacles—and our work with them to remove such obstacles—that we move into deeper union with God.

>>>>>>>>>>>

Here's another beatitude I think Jesus would add to the list. Blessed are the psychotic.

As a minister in an urban setting, I come into contact with my fair share of people with signs of severe mental illness. Saucy J, for example, told me she had an earpiece with the Secret Service and Beyoncé on speed dial. The next morning, I found her sleeping on the steps of our church. I offered to walk her over to the homeless drop-in center a few blocks away, but she said she needed to go meet some high-level government officials and took off in the other direction.

A few years ago, I met someone who thought he was the president of the United States. He asked me to pray for him as he was feeling the weight of the office. I was more than happy to pray for the state of our nation and ask that God grant him wisdom in leadership and decision-making. He found the church's phone number and has been calling me about once a month for prayer ever since.

Saucy J and the president are obviously experiencing psychosis, a serious lack of connection to reality. But it's not always so obvious. People who present as psychotic often speak of spiritual matters. It's hard to know whether the person is having a religious delusion, a legitimate religious experience, or both.

During my Tuesday blessings, one man came up to me and asked if I knew who he was. I racked my brain, trying to place him, but to no avail. Feeling embarrassed, I had to admit I didn't recognize him. "You really don't know who I am? I can't believe you don't recognize me. I'm Origin! The Virgin Mary appeared to me four times and told me she'd marry me when I got to heaven." Continued conversation confirmed that "Origin" was not fully grounded in reality. But who am I to say that he's wrong about the visits of the Virgin Mary? Mary has appeared to many people throughout history, including me. When I talk to her during my personal prayer time, she sometimes shows up with big hair and a Staten Island accent, wearing a blue satin dress, and smoking a cigarette. (Hopefully you don't think I'm psychotic too.)

The point is I've had people who seem mentally ill tell me about their visions. Some tell me they have the gift of prophecy or can discern spiritual evil in others.

They usually don't make complete sense to me. But that doesn't mean God is not active in them. Or hasn't gifted them in a uniquely spiritual way. One such person who claimed to be a prophet told me to "stay safe and leave New York City." A global pandemic hit the city hard three months later.

The Beatitudes show us that people in need of God because of their own vulnerability are in a prime position to be blessed. Contrast the first beatitude, "Blessed are you who are poor, for yours is the kingdom of God," with this later verse in Luke: "Indeed, it is easier for a camel to go through the eye of a needle than for someone who is rich to enter the kingdom of God." According to this logic, the more vulnerable you are—or make yourself to be—the easier it is for you to receive God's grace. And this isn't just about money. If we are rich in anything, even in our own talents and abilities, the temptation is to rely on those talents and abilities exclusively without making room for God's grace. The pathway for grace lies in vulnerability.

Whether vulnerability comes from an external force, such as poverty or tragedy, or an internal force, such as humility or repentance, God has a way of getting in there. Vulnerability is scary, yet it's what allows us to be touched so deeply by the divine. And what could make a person more vulnerable than a vulnerability in the brain?

This all leads me to another definition of *blessing*: connection to God. To be blessed is to be connected to God. This shows up in a variety of contexts. Sometimes we have a felt connection to God that is accompanied by laughter and joy. Sometimes it's serenity and peace. And sometimes we experience God in the midst of our tears. Blessed are those who mourn.

This is not to say that we can ever romanticize psychosis or poverty or illness or any kind of affliction. Afflictions are meant to be healed, and God is the source of healing, in both this life and the next. Jesus remains with the vulnerable and in our vulnerabilities, providing a window into his nature of suffering love and desire to draw us into his intimate embrace.

So, yes. Blessed are those with psychosis. Blessed are those in pain. Blessed are those who feel deeply. And blessed are all those brave enough to admit any kind of weakness, for they see—and shall see—God.

>>>>>>>>>>>>

Ready for another beatitude? Blessed are those who don't want a blessing but receive it anyway.

A few years into this ministry, I noticed a trend. The #MeToo movement was gaining traction, and I started to hear from more and more women about sexual harassment, sexual abuse, and sexual assault. Some wanted prayer for a friend or family member who had suffered in one of these ways. Some wanted to lament a sex scandal in the news, often saying "I can't believe it" in one breath and "I'm not surprised" in the next. (I can relate.) And some were brave enough to confide in me their own experience of sexual harm in the hopes that I could offer a compassionate word, invoke God's healing presence, or simply bear witness to their pain.

One of these survivors wanted me to bear witness to something more: her faith and God's miraculous working in her life. She had fallen away from Christianity for a decade or so and then returned to church, prayer, and Scripture. Almost immediately, however, she began remembering an incident of childhood sexual abuse that she had repressed. It was as if the more she sought after God, the more the memories surfaced. This, of course, brought with it a world of hurt, confusion, and the need for therapy. But she knew God was the one bringing it to light, and God was the one to help her heal. Healing could only begin by standing in the place of pain.

This woman's experience is not unique. As we walk in the light, God brings things to light, including ugly truths. These truths may be about ourselves, our past, our circumstances, or even the underbelly of society. Many champions of social justice are moved to take up their cause because God gives them eyes to see and the courage to not look away. This is a type of blessing that I've received and one that I never wanted. But if it's from God, it's a blessing whether you like it or not.

In my last year of seminary, I started receiving horrific visions in my dreams and during my prayer time. They were images of child rape and forced prostitution. I remember going to the dentist during this time, and on the TV in the waiting room was a talk show featuring a woman from California who was prostituted by her parents at age eleven. I asked the receptionist to change the channel. When I went to the gym, I got on the elliptical machine and found a magazine opened to an article about sex trafficking in Mexico. It included a picture of women walking in a big circle in a parking lot while men stood on the outside, deciding which one to pick. I read the first paragraph and had to stop. I knew the way these things were coming to my attention was not mere coincidence. It was a message from God—and one I chose to ignore.

Fast forward nearly two years, and the Holy Spirit hadn't let up. The dreams had stopped, but they were replaced by a nagging voice. As part of my ministry as a parish priest, I had been taking on more and more work at a homeless shelter. But I could feel God saying, "That's not what I'm asking of you." I knew I couldn't substitute one area of need for another. As I like to tell my parishioners, "Not every good deed has our name on it. But we serve a God who calls us by name." God has very specific things for each of us to do, including ways of engaging brokenness in the world. I knew God was calling me to explore the issue of human trafficking and to figure out what I could do about it. So with a sense of resignation,

I began my research. I felt outrage at the ugliness of the issue, despair over its magnitude, and a sense of frustrated urgency to do something while not knowing what that could possibly be. Yet the more informed I became, the more empowered I felt. I began to make connections with other people passionate about the issue, and we started forming anti-trafficking ministries.

Years later, the relationships I'd formed through partnering with various nonprofits, religious groups, and survivors of trafficking gave me the idea for a major project: a pilgrimage, of sorts, through New York City with the Episcopal Diocese of New York Task Force Against Human Trafficking. We called it Stations of the Cross for Sex Trafficking Survivors. The traditional Stations of the Cross is a devotional journey that depicts scenes from the last day of Christ's life. Christians around the world, in a variety of traditions, participate in the Stations of the Cross during Holy Week, the week leading up to Easter. Prayers and images help the faithful contemplate the events of Good Friday.

For our Stations of the Cross for Sex Trafficking Survivors, we superimposed the plight of people trafficked for sex on the Passion narratives, which tell Jesus's story of suffering. Some stations we visited were places where victims are recruited or trafficked, such as Port Authority Bus Terminal. Others were places where survivors experience healing and justice, such as a center for LGBTQ youth and a human trafficking intervention court. At each station, we gathered outside to offer prayers and hear from a speaker, including survivor-advocates, service providers, and other experts. We used the event to raise awareness about what sex trafficking looks like in New York City and point to the need for a legislative solution that would decriminalize people bought and sold in the sex trade while continuing to criminalize their exploiters. One of the greatest blessings was having a reporter from the BBC join us to expand the reach of our efforts to raise awareness. She produced a radio broadcast heard by millions around the world on Good Friday and again on Easter Sunday.

The fight against human trafficking is now a cause very close to my heart. Becoming involved in anti-trafficking activism and ministry is a blessing I didn't want—and even resisted—but one that came to me nonetheless. It's a blessing that has born real fruit, which further affirms that it's from God. I never dreamed I would have much of an impact, but God's "power at work within us is able to accomplish abundantly far more than all we can ask or imagine."

I once spoke about my anti-trafficking efforts to a man who stopped for prayer and a blessing on the sidewalk. He had become one of my Tuesday-morning regulars and was interested in learning about the ministries of my church. At the time, we had just formed a partnership with the leading policy organization in the United States seeking to end the commercial sexual exploitation of children, known as ECPAT-USA. Part of their work involves developing training for hotel staff to recognize the signs of child sex trafficking on hotel property. So I organized teams of parishioners to visit the many hotels in Midtown Manhattan. We went around encouraging hotel management to utilize ECPAT-USA's training materials and also post the human trafficking hotline number. When I told the man who stopped for prayer about this initiative, he was shocked to learn how rampant trafficking is in our country and in our city, how young the victims are, and how easy it is for traffickers to get away with it.

So he started doing research. Each week, he'd show up more outraged and incredulous than the last, telling me about another article he'd read on the subject. He was going through the same pattern of reactions I had experienced over the years as I'd become more aware of and pained by the realities of trafficking.

It turned out this man was a journalist, and he decided to write an article of his own. His first piece in the *New York Times* was "Bill Seeks to Enlist New York Hotels to Help Fight Sex Trafficking." He ran with the hotel angle in his article and highlighted the church's outreach ministry to Midtown hotels. Since then, New York State has made it a law that hotels display the trafficking hotline number on cards in every room so victims might call for help. Proposed legislation mandating trafficking recognition training for hotel employees will hopefully pass next.

You never know how God will use the encounters between two strangers seeking to do good. Strangers who may become friends, and even partners in ministry, with an unconventional story about how they met. God gave us both eyes to see and the courage to not look away so that we might shine some light on a social ill that thrives in darkness.

The apostle Paul writes that "everything exposed by the light becomes visible, for everything that becomes visible is light." I've never been able to quite wrap my mind around this verse, but I take it to mean that God can redeem even the gravest and most sinful situation, as long as it comes out of shadows and into the healing light of Christ. We're in a time when all manner of hate and perversion and oppression are coming to light. All sorts of victims and survivors and allies are speaking up. Most women I've talked to have had one or more #MeToo moments of varying degrees. I certainly have. The sins of white supremacy are finally coming to the fore for many white people as undeniable realities of the present, not just problems of the past.

This is a season to lay claim to Paul's words. To bring the ugly truth face to face with the one who calls himself *the* Truth, and the Way, and the Life. His light burns brightly in the darkest corners of our lives and in the world. We've been given a beacon of hope, a call to look at what's illuminated, and an invitation to fan the flame.

6

WILL SOMEBODY BLESS ME?

Every once in a while, I meet someone who wants to pray for me rather than having it the other way around. They usually approach me with great enthusiasm, surprised and delighted to see someone who appears to be all in for Jesus, which I am. I love it when this happens. We might talk about the goodness of God, life in Christ, and whatever spiritual stories they wish to share. Then I heartily welcome their prayers, which generally end up being a request for God to fill me with the Spirit and bless my ministry. Amen.

One day, I had one of these familiar encounters but with an unexpected twist. A woman opened her prayer by asking God to forgive me and cleanse me, citing 1 John 1:9. She didn't quote this verse of Scripture, but I know it by heart. It's in the *Episcopal Book of Common Prayer*, and we say it in services during Lent: "If we confess our sins, God who is faithful and just will forgive us our sins and cleanse us from all unrighteousness."

Okay, I thought; I didn't express a need for forgiveness to this woman, but I could get on board with that. Then she asked Jesus to reveal anything in me that is not of him so that I might be *further* cleansed.

For a second, I thought of a scene in the movie *Come Sunday*, which is a true story about a fundamentalist pastor who loses his megachurch because he tells his congregation that hell doesn't exist. Almost everyone walks out on him, and his bishop declares him a heretic. Given this perceived apostasy by the church community, one of his former congregation members thinks the devil must be involved. She approaches his wife in the supermarket, asks to pray for her, and then essentially tries to cast out a demon.

Was this woman on the sidewalk trying to cast something out of me? Did she think I was a heretic? *I very well might be*, I thought, but that was beside the point. I waited a bit nervously as she prayed, wondering when the exorcism might begin. But she didn't go to demons or the devil. Still within the context of prayer, she offered an analogy that put my mind at ease. We all pick up dirt without even realizing it, she said. We can look down at our jeans and notice a stain and not know where it came from. I agree that we can likewise pick up sinful behaviors unintentionally. Father, forgive us, for we know not what we do.

The rest of the woman's prayer was beautiful. I prayed for her too, and the whole experience ended up being the highlight of my day. It also caused me to reflect on a few sins I'd been struggling with but hadn't acknowledged before God. There were plenty of stains on my jeans, and I sorely needed God to scrub them away.

So why had I been so sensitive to this woman seeking God's forgiveness on my behalf? At least initially? As I mentioned, I hadn't asked her to do this, so there's that. Yet I believe that repentance and forgiveness are integral to the good news of salvation in Jesus Christ. And while it's not exactly the same thing as the woman asking God to forgive me, I pronounce God's forgiveness over people all the time. Every Sunday, after the congregation reads a general confession in worship, I say a version of the following: "The Almighty and merciful Lord grant you absolution and remission of all your sins, true repentance, amendment of life, and the grace and consolation of his Holy Spirit."

Not long after this woman prayed that I might be purged of my sin, I heard someone's confession. While we do the general confession in church, some people want to make a more personal confession in private. This is done in the context of a brief service called the rite of reconciliation of a penitent. You won't find a confessional booth in many Episcopal churches, including mine. So I use a small chapel for the rite of reconciliation. I sit side by side with the person making their confession, and we face the altar. The whole thing takes about an hour because it includes some counseling and discussion about the specific sins confessed.

The language in the rite of reconciliation includes another memorable line from our prayer book. After hearing the penitent's confession and proclaiming words of absolution, the priest concludes the service by saying "Go in peace, and pray for me, a sinner." I like this ending because it so blatantly recognizes the fact that we all sin. It reminds me that *I* sin and that there's freedom in saying I'm a sinner. Owning my sin creates space for death to self, a blow to pride, and constant renewal through contrition and grace.

In reflecting on these two experiences together—having a stranger ask God to forgive my sins and hearing a parishioner's confession—I remembered a helpful image. I once read that we are like cats, and God sometimes pets us against the grain of our fur. Being pet in the wrong direction is something most cats can't stand. If you have a cat in your life, try it sometime and see what happens. So when it's God doing the petting, and when I'm the cat, the only solution is to turn around and face the other direction. The woman who prayed for God to cleanse me and point out my sin? She definitely caused me to bristle. But she also caused me to repent, which literally means to turn around, to turn away from those things that are death-dealing and face God, who is life-giving.

My favorite way to think about sin—yes, I actually have a favorite way of thinking about sin—is in terms of brokenness and our need for healing and restoration because we are so fallible. Jesus is the Great Physician. Christ is the healer. He heals the sin-sick soul, and he makes the wounded whole. We all stray, we all get lost, and we all need to be found time and time again. Whether it's because of what we've done, when we've sinned, or what's been done to us, when we've been sinned against, or a combination of both, sin breaks things. It infects. It stains. Repairing or healing or cleansing sin—take your pick of metaphor—requires naming it, whether it's our sin or the sin of others.

Yet we all can be slow to name the sin in our lives. Contemplating our sins—really sitting with them—is not a fashionable thing to do. If we go to church, we may be fine with saying the more vague, general confession with the rest of the congregation on Sundays. We may have an easy time admitting that humanity, as a whole, is sinful and broken. We might even acknowledge that we, as individuals, sin every day. But taking a hard look at the places where I or you, specifically, need to change? That doesn't come so easily. If we're not breaking laws or actively setting out to hurt people, we might think we're doing fine. But the more insidious sin—the self-righteous thought, the passive-aggressive comment, the despairing attitude, the blind participation in systems of injustice— can be just as harmful as the outwardly obvious sins, if not more.

Repentance is a way of acknowledging our need for Jesus. It creates the space for him to come in and do his transformative work in our hearts. It's opening ourselves up to receive God's grace. It's saying "I'm sorry, God, *and* I want help with this area of my life, *and* I intend to live differently than I have been." Then we go out and try to live in this new way as the new creations God intended us to be.

I hadn't realized it right away, but that woman was right. I needed to repent. My impatience was at an all-time high because I was super-stressed and spending less time in prayer. Factor in my type AAA personality, and I'd been acting like a real know-it-all. Jesus not only heals the grand rift between humanity and God. He heals our blind spots, helping us see those things we need to change. And then he gives us the healing grace to change them. It might not be enough grace to kick that sin to the curb overnight, once and for all. But it will be enough for today. God's grace is always sufficient for today.

>>>>>>>>>>>>

I stopped my sidewalk ministry completely when the coronavirus broke out. Even as lockdowns began to lift, many people were wary of having interactions that weren't absolutely necessary. Not that there were many people around for me to talk to anyway. Our neighborhood was eerily desolate, and Midtown Manhattan in general was a ghost town compared to its former self. Next to no commuters, vacant office buildings, closed businesses (if not shuttered completely), and certainly no tourists.

But during this time, I received emails from a few of my regulars who were working from home.

"Such strange times; can't think of a time when God is more needed."

"Never thought I would actually miss commuting into the city."

"Certainly look forward to being able to receive a blessing and hug from you. Who thought hugs and handshakes would be so taken for granted?"

"For the 'ask for a blessing' of the week, I would like to pray for all those who will suffer economic hardship because of the effects of the pandemic—that they will keep faith and find work and relief as soon as possible."

"Can I call you? I need a prayer."

The answer to that last one was "Yes, please do." Praying on the phone is not a frequent practice for me, but I'm still a fan because of my first experience calling someone for prayer.

One night during college, I watched a movie that disturbed me greatly. It followed the downward spiral of various characters through the horrors of drug addiction and crazed desperation. When it was over, I felt spiritually polluted, like I had taken in something I shouldn't have.

I had trouble sleeping that night, and the film still haunted me the next day. After my morning class, I went directly to a campus phone outside the lecture hall and called a friend from high school. This was before cell phones—at least before *I* had a cell phone—and I'm so grateful she picked up. "Will you please pray for me?" I asked. "I saw this awful movie last night and can't get the images out of my head."

In one of the most meaningful moments of our friendship, she prayed for me right then and there over the phone. Eyes closed tight, clutching the receiver, and hanging on her every word, I learned that the power of prayer goes beyond our attempts to influence God. It's a power that cuts to the core of our being with a mix of compassion, intimacy, and hope. I don't remember what she said, but I remember the way she made me feel: safe, at peace, loved by God. It's a gift I've tried to pass on ever since.

As usual, offering this gift was my intention when I resumed my blessings on the street after my initial pandemic hiatus. It had been nearly four months since I'd stood out there with my chalkboard. Foot traffic had picked up a bit, although it was a far cry from the usual hustle and bustle. I donned a mask that matched my stole, and I drew an X with sidewalk chalk to show people where to stand, six feet away.

It didn't take long before a bus pulled up right in front of me. There were no people on the bus, even though it was technically rush hour, so the driver stepped out to chat for a few minutes while the bus idled. Unsurprisingly, he said he was stressed. He was concerned about keeping himself and his family safe from COVID-19. He had endured a lot of mistreatment on the job and even assaults from passengers. He was exhausted, and he looked it.

I asked him how he was coping with it all. His response demonstrated a deep faith. He said he tries to be in "prayer mode" throughout the day, especially when driving the bus. He recites verses from Psalm 91, which is all about God's protection: "For he will command his angels concerning you to guard you in all your ways. On their hands they will bear you up, so that you will not dash your foot against a stone." And, the bus driver said, he knows that he will emerge stronger from this in the end.

I spoke some words of encouragement, grounded in our shared faith, and then I gave him a blessing. He went on his way, hopefully feeling a little better and a little more at peace than before. I certainly did. Knowing that he was out there serving our city, I started to trust in the truth of his words: that we would all emerge stronger from this in the end.

As I watched the bus drive away, I realized that I finally felt like a New Yorker. I've heard that it takes about ten years of living here for a transplant like myself to earn that title. Other markers might be when you see a rat on the subway tracks and think nothing of it. Or you no longer notice the poor production quality of the TV station that broadcasts local news twenty-four hours a day. Those were both true for me. But calling myself a full-fledged New Yorker? Even after hitting that ten-year mark, it still never felt right to me—until, that is, I lived in New York City through a pandemic.

Many people fled the city, and I don't begrudge them one bit. My husband and I needed to stay for our jobs, so we hunkered down. It wasn't safe to ride the subway or walk around after dark. Outdoor activities were limited, everything that draws people to New York City was shut down, and we joined the throngs of people stuck inside their apartments. In the middle of deep health, economic, and social crises, we mourned the incredible losses all around us.

But we felt good about spending our money to support our local economy. We took groceries to people in need. We joined in Black Lives Matter marches and the daily 7:00 p.m. cheer across New York City for frontline workers. Soon I had the church bells timed to go off at 7:00 p.m. too. And, of course, I was doing my best to be a spiritual leader for my congregation during dark and trying times, dealing with COVID-19-related deaths, hospitalizations, and people suffering at home.

This all led me to finally feel comfortable claiming my status as a New Yorker. It was about communal identity forged through adversity. While we are not necessarily defined by what we've been through or what has happened to us in this life, we can own what we have overcome. And when you have persevered through a collective experience, you feel a connection to those with whom you've shared that experience.

The bus driver who stopped to talk to me didn't just share my identity as a Christian. He shared my identity as a New Yorker. I knew it when I looked in his eyes. We exchanged empathy for one another before even opening our mouths. And while I know the details of our experiences differed—and that my experience of the pandemic could be described as almost cushy compared to that of many others in the city—there was a kindred connection underlying our encounter. As I watched the bus driver pull away from the curb, I felt such love for my city. I felt energized. Come get yourself a blessing, New York!

>>>>>>>>>>>>

Too bad no one else stopped for twenty minutes. Like I said, no hustle, no bustle. I stood there by myself, wondering if I should just call it a day.

But just as I was about to close up shop, my passion sufficiently waned, along came one of the most colorful characters I've met in this ministry. She wore a mask that pictured a drawing of the Virgin Mary with the words "Our Lady of the Savior." I thought it was fantastic. Right off the bat, I knew this would be a longer conversation than normal.

The woman was so excited to see me. She started digging in her purse to show me some rosary beads while simultaneously launching into her life story. I didn't mind. At that point in the pandemic, we all had been so deprived of face-to-face conversation that any in-person interaction felt like a precious moment we were reluctant to end. Plus, we obviously had a shared love of witnessing to the power of God, so I knew we'd both come away spiritually uplifted.

With a true flair for the dramatic, this woman stressed the many hardships she'd overcome only by God's grace. I tried to match a fraction of her energy in affirming her testimony, cheering her on with "Praise God!" and "Thank you, Jesus!" All the while, I was subtly moving my feet to inch backward and sideways, as if doing a foxtrot, because her mask kept slipping, and she was completely disregarding my X on the sidewalk. She described Jesus as "my Lord and my Love," while bringing her hands to her heart and turning her head to the side, eyes closed. *How touching*, I thought as I took another step sideways.

And then she took a complete left turn, in my mind at least. She said that she prayed Jesus would give her just a little of the pain he experienced on the cross. This was a new one for me, especially given all the suffering going on in our city. It had only been a matter of weeks since hospitals, as well as morgues, had been completely overrun. And she was asking to suffer?

Suffering is certainly a pervasive theme in Scripture, just as it is in life. It can help a great deal to see that our own pain is consistent with, and perhaps even in some way prescribed by, the biblical narrative we claim as our own. Rather than asking Jesus to take away our pain, we can ask him to enter into it. We've got divine company in our pain, and that's a comfort.

But entering into *his* pain? Inviting his suffering into our lives? That seems a bit scary, if not masochistic. It goes beyond a willingness to suffer for Christ. It also harkens back to a time when some Christians would practice self-mortification as a form of penance. (Too bad the body-positive movement wasn't around then.)

I can't speak to what this woman meant, exactly, by her prayer for pain. But her deep devotion to Jesus reminded me that his pain was an expression of his deep devotion to us. Praying to receive his pain could be praying to receive his heart—a heart that breaks over injustice and is moved to act in love.

Two saints with the heart of Jesus came to mind. Mother Teresa often spoke about serving people in need until it hurts. While it's true that serving usually makes us feel good, sometimes it's not about the good feeling at all. Eventually, you go so deep into service and solidarity with those who are suffering that you go beyond the pain it causes you. At that point, the only thing left is love. This is what Mother Teresa did for the impoverished in the slums of Calcutta. This is what God did for us all in Jesus Christ.

The other saint is Ignatius of Loyola, who famously prayed to Mary, "Place me with your Son." In response, he received a vision not of Jesus hanging on the cross but of Jesus carrying the cross. He interpreted it as a call to serve.

"Place me with your Son." This was a prayer I could get behind and one that I expanded upon later that day while seated at my desk:

> Place me with your Son.
> Knowing it will sometimes hurt, place me with your Son.
> Knowing it's what the world needs, place me with your Son.
> Knowing I'll have abundant life, place me with your Son.
> Place me with your Son, my Lord and my Love.

After typing up this prayer, I hit *print* on the computer, cut out the prayer with scissors to create a little slip of paper, and sat down with it in the church. Given my Protestant sensibilities, I offered this prayer to God rather than to Mary. The image I received was of Jesus reading from the scroll of Isaiah in the synagogue: "The Spirit of the Lord is upon me, because he has anointed me to bring good news to the poor."

The idea of being placed with Jesus in the synagogue turned out to be pretty timely for me. Pandemic burnout had set in, and my job as a parish priest was harder than I could have ever imagined. People were hurting. I was caught in a flurry of phone calls and emails, with no ability to see any of the individuals in person. Beyond that, I had to rely on Zoom meetings and mass communications to meet my congregation in their pain. I was churning out spiritual content in e-blasts and video reflections, trying to deliver messages of hope and encouragement that also responded to injustices brought into sharp relief by the murder of George Floyd and the disproportionate effects of the pandemic on people of color. All the while, I was tackling the very mundane yet critical tasks of fighting with Verizon to upgrade the church's internet speed, getting the right AV equipment installed in the sanctuary so people could stream worship services on YouTube, researching the ever-changing safety protocols to keep my staff safe, and navigating the Paycheck Protection Program. Some days, I had an escapist urge to run away from it all. Not that I ever would, but it sure did help to meet fellow Christians—including the two I met that day—who told me about their love of God.

Truth be told, it also helps to meet the skeptics and the seekers, people of different faiths and no faith at all. I'm grateful both for those who thank me and those who call me to repentance. This ministry is one of the greatest blessings of my life because of the people who make it up.

>>>>>>>>>>>

"I'm an atheist. My girlfriend is a Christian. And we can't even talk about religion without her bursting into tears. Can you help?" This man was not looking for a prayer, and his request required more than a brief conversation on the street. So he made an appointment and came to see me in the office.

The story he shared about himself and his girlfriend ended up being a familiar fact pattern—one I knew well because I had been that girlfriend. Brought up fundamentalist. Always taught I had to marry a Christian so as not to be "unequally yoked." Started dating a guy in college who had been raised Catholic but identified as agnostic. Felt torn about dating him, attacked when he asked questions about my faith beliefs, intolerant of even listening to his beliefs, and ultimately sad and fearful that he would end up in hell. I was frequently bursting into tears too.

Not so ironically, my boyfriend became even more resistant to Christianity. My attempts to convert him didn't help either. My behavior was immature, yet my pain and fear were very real. They stemmed from a heartfelt theological belief that only Christians go to heaven. I've long since abandoned that belief because I've become convinced through my own soul-searching, exposure to people of different cultures and religions, and study of Scripture, theology, and church history that God doesn't operate that way. But back then, I clung to this belief from my childhood. I couldn't even entertain a thought that challenged it.

So when this man I met on the street sat in my office and described his situation, I realized what he needed most was to feel heard. He didn't feel heard by his girlfriend, just as my boyfriend hadn't felt heard by me. This time I listened, and I listened deeply.

It turned out he wasn't as much of an atheist as he thought. While he didn't speak explicitly in spiritual terms, he talked about healing, personal transformation, and what I identified as the movement of God in his life. I answered his questions about Jesus and the church. We discussed differences among Christian denominations. He said he wanted to come to Bible study. While he never made it to that, he's become a regular member of my congregation.

As for that college boyfriend of mine? I married him. We both have deep and meaningful relationships with Jesus and a Christ-centered marriage, in large part because of the Episcopal Church. This could only happen after I let go of my distress over his salvation and was able to honor where he was on his spiritual journey. It turned out the historical Jesus—the man who was rebellious, revolutionary, and called for social justice in a world where his people were oppressed—held great appeal for my husband. As did the power of our church's community to bring together people of different ages, backgrounds, beliefs, ethnicities, and socioeconomic status. There's a saying I learned in the Episcopal Church: "Belong before you believe." That's what happened with my husband. I just needed to get out of the way.

The desire to evangelize is obviously still with me, with much thanks to the faith tradition of my childhood and the importance it places on Christian witness. My emphasis is less on conversion, however, and more in line with the mission of Canterbury Cathedral, the mother church of the Anglican Communion. That, quite simply, is "to show people Jesus." Confess him with a quiet confidence in his love, proclaim the goodness of his grace all around us, and trust that one day every knee shall bow and every tongue confess that Jesus Christ is Lord.

>>>>>>>>>>>>

So about that, confessing Jesus Christ as Lord. Some Christians—heck, probably a fair number of Christians—aren't fully on board with this. I know because I've met several. One day, a woman walked up to me on the sidewalk and, with a knowing look in her eye, folded her arms across her chest, hands resting on opposite shoulders. This is a position people sometimes assume in church when they come forward during Communion. It indicates they'd like to receive a blessing instead of the bread and the wine. We exchanged a smile over this shared understanding of a small ritual. I asked if she was an Episcopalian, and, indeed, she was.

She had been steeped in the church, she said, yet she needed a prayer for wavering faith. She was no longer sure that Jesus was the Son of God. We prayed that this time of doubt would energize her spiritual journey and that God would ultimately restore her faith. After all, faith in God can only come from God. It's a gift from on high.

It's also a gift that some say they want but have never received. During my time as a hospital chaplain, I spoke with a few patients who said they wished they had faith but just didn't. I told them that even the desire for faith constituted some level of faith itself.

Still, their situation felt sad and unfair to me because I couldn't lose my faith even if I tried. God is in my face all the time. I shared this sentiment with my chaplaincy supervisor at the hospital, a wise rabbi. He responded, "Why do you think God made it that way?" As in, why did God make it easier for some people to have faith than others?

My answer was not as important as my acceptance of the question's premise. Yes, by God's design, some people have an easier time receiving the gift of faith. We can't all be Moses at the burning bush. Other factors that make it easier or harder to receive faith can include natural inclination, upbringing, a penchant for theological study, and all manner of life experience. Not to mention the fact that we all live in a post-Enlightenment world. For the vast majority of human history, God's existence was never in question. Not so today. Yet even for those who believe in God and ascribe to a religious tradition, many waver in their faith at some point or another. That may be by God's design, too, in order to lead them into a stronger, more mature faith in the long run. The common struggle to have faith or keep the faith is one reason we need faith leaders and faith communities to build each other up and shepherd each other along. It also means that faith, while a gift, is not an all-or-nothing gift. It's something we cultivate and nurture. It takes effort and implies action. Having faith includes being faithful to God in how we live.

When it comes to being faithful in prayer, there's a saying that "praying shapes believing." While these words are typically used to uphold the centrality of worship in the life of the church, they also speak to the personal beliefs of individuals. Praying shapes the way we see God because prayer gives God access to our hearts in a way that nothing else can. We might offer prayers written by our spiritual ancestors, confess our deepest desires and darkest secrets, or sit silently when we are speechless with grief or worry, allowing the Holy Spirit to intercede on our behalf "with sighs too deep for words." Whether our prayers flow from a sure and certain hope or arise from a place of searching and doubt, God uses them. Through our prayers, God touches our inmost being and, over time, reveals the truth about God's nature.

In the Gospel of Mark, a man cries out to Jesus, "I believe; help my unbelief!" Then Jesus heals his son. This means that no matter where we are in our faith—no matter how frail, fractured, or rock solid it may be—God is faithful to us. I wish I knew what happened with that woman who doubted Jesus's divinity. When I learn of someone who drifts away from their faith, my heart breaks just a little. At the same time, and despite the fact that God is up in my face, there are moments when I start to drift too. I think, *Is this Jesus thing baloney? Am I living a lie? Have I really devoted my life to the church? I believe; help my unbelief!*

I got a tattoo a few years ago. It's a small cross on the inside of my forearm. I never wanted the cross to be upside down, regardless of what position my arm was in, as an upside-down cross is bad mojo. So I had to pick a cross that sort of resembled a plus sign. I went with a cross-crosslet, which is a cross with a crossbar near the end of each arm of the cross. It's like four normal (or Latin) crosses stuck together in the middle. A common interpretation is that it represents the four evangelists—Matthew, Mark, Luke, and John—taking the gospel into the world. This cross was perfect for me, and I was in love with my new tattoo.

Literally one week after getting it, however, I couldn't believe what I'd done. I was putting together some materials for a Sunday school craft that involved the Episcopal flag, and I saw the cross-crosslet. *Nine* of them, in fact. I hadn't even realized that this cross was on my denomination's flag! I felt like such a moron, such a fangirl. *Rah, rah, Episcopal Church!* Uh, no.

But while I never would have gotten that tattoo had I known, I'm now so glad I did. As one of my friends joked, "Now you're branded!" It's true, and reminiscent of the "branding" we receive in baptism—marked as Christ's own forever. Whenever my faith in God or my faith in myself starts to get shaky, I look at that cross on my arm. I remember that faith is not only a gift. It's a choice. It's a loving response to God, who first loved me.

This is what I mean about choosing faith. Circumstances come about, actions are taken—by us and others, both good and bad. Events happen that are in and out of our control. Some relationships fail, while others flourish. We can look back on all these things and see God somewhere in their midst. Or not. We can choose to see the secular shot through with the sacred. Or not.

I choose the former. I choose to see God's hand at work in our lives, guiding us to do what is right, bringing good out of bad, and, to paraphrase Martin Luther King Jr., bending the arc of the moral universe toward justice. I choose to see blessings in disguise. I choose to see God weeping with us, rejoicing with us, conforming us to Christ through the struggles and the celebrations, helping us to hold on to the lessons and let go of the baggage. I choose faith. I choose life. And I choose to come alongside others so they may find the same.

》》》》》》》》》》》

When I stand in front of my church to offer blessings, I often spend a few minutes fixating on a shadow. On most days, our church steeple casts a large shadow on the furniture store directly across the street. The clear outline of the cross takes shape above a massive display window. I feel proud of that shadow, and held within it, as I stand there on the sidewalk. "Whoever dwells in the shelter of the Most High will rest in the shadow of the Almighty."

It's no surprise that I'm drawn to the places where church meets world. There's something so uniquely beautiful, for example, about a funeral procession that spills out from the church onto the street. Pallbearers carry the casket down the steps and load it into the hearse while a priest offers prayers. Then the priest pronounces a final blessing over the deceased, making the sign of the cross before the door to the hearse is closed. Family members cry, hug, and share words of consolation born out of their faith in God and assurance of eternal life. Random people on the sidewalk will often stop for this brief ritual, looking on or bowing their heads in reverence. For a moment, everyone is truly standing on holy ground. Then a few minutes later, the busy street is back to normal.

Of course, there's more to church meeting world than explicitly religious actions taken in public spaces. It happens wherever the good news is proclaimed in word or deed—wherever Christians have spilled out of the church to spread the kingdom of God. The thing about God's house—our church home—is that we're not meant to stay there. We come in on Sundays to nurture our faith so that we can live it out the rest of the week. We come in to build one another up in the body of Christ so we can be Christ's hands and feet in the world. We come in to be nourished in worship and the Eucharist so we can show hungry people where to find spiritual food, and living water, and saving grace.

When I started this ministry, my goal was to connect the church to the world by simply stepping a few feet outside the front doors. I wanted to evangelize in a nonthreatening way. I wanted to speak good news into people's lives, especially through prayer. I wanted to affirm God's love for as many people as possible. All these things still ring true, as loud as church bells on a Sunday morning. What I never expected was how much blessing I would get back.

Remember the kind of humility that comes with receiving a big award? The feeling of undeservedness mixed with gratitude? Just as I'm humbled by the gift of God's grace, I'm humbled by the gift of this ministry. I'm humbled by ways that people reveal God—in themselves, in me, in our interaction. With humor, in sorrow, or by simply being open. When the premise and purpose of meeting a stranger is to share a sacred moment, God comes on the scene. Spiritual connection is made and spiritual hunger is met.

Spiritual hunger is the only type of hunger that grows when it's satisfied. We long for God, God meets the longing, and God keeps us wanting more. The entire time I've been out there on the sidewalk, seeking to share spiritual food, I'm the one who's been fed. It's part of the reason I keep going back. So here's one final definition of *blessing*: the act of offering and receiving spiritual nourishment through an encounter in God's name.

At the end of every service of Holy Eucharist, there is a prayer that everyone says together after receiving the bread and the wine. It's a prayer of thanksgiving for being fed with spiritual food and a prayer for strength and courage to love and serve God as we go forth into the world. We are fed so that we can feed others. We are blessed so that we can bless others. This is my prayer for you. If you have found spiritual nourishment in these pages, may you be emboldened to go out into the world to love, serve, feed, and bless.

7

A CRASH COURSE IN BLESSING

We all want to be there for others through highs and lows, through thick and thin. God wants to be there for them too, just like God wants to be there for you. And here's the beautiful thing: you and God can do this together. That's what blessing others is all about—coming together with God in support of another person.

Sound appealing? Scary? Both? I have some tips to get you going. I call them *lessons from a seminarian*. First things first, though: I'm not asking you to set up a blessing booth on the sidewalk. Although if you're interested in that, let me know, and I'll definitely come join you. I'm also not asking you to talk to strangers, much less pray for them in public. But again, I'm here if you need me.

Simply consider what it might look like for you to bless someone—someone you know—by providing spiritual support. This can happen in conversation or through offering a prayer aloud on their behalf. Maybe you've been in a situation similar to one of these.

A friend calls you on the phone to talk about something that's stressing them out.

You're celebrating a family member's accomplishment and want to mark the occasion with a blessing or prayer.

You want to connect with your teen, who seems hard to talk to these days.

Someone in your book group, friend group, or church group shares that they're going through a tough time.

Maybe being in a situation like this made you feel awkward, unsure, or lacking in the prayers or spiritual words for such an encounter. Maybe you've wished a pastor or priest or rabbi were present. Surely a member of the clergy—even a seminary student—would know what to say or do, right?

Actually, sometimes clergy and seminarians don't know what to say or do either, but training for the pastorate or priesthood does give us some practice talking to people about spiritual stuff. The most important part of a seminary education, in my opinion, doesn't happen in the classroom. It happens in the hospital. As a requirement for graduation and ordination, I spent one summer as an interfaith hospital chaplain in a program called Clinical Pastoral Education (CPE). Here's the scary thing about CPE. You start visiting patients right off the bat, going by the title *chaplain* before you have any clue what you're doing.

For someone who knows very little about the Boy Scouts but lives by their motto—"Be prepared"—I felt thrown into the deep end without knowing how to swim. The first week of CPE, I was assigned to the oncology and pediatric units. In no way did I feel ready to act as a chaplain to people with cancer or sick children and their parents. But there was no way around it. The only way to learn the skills of the job is to practice them over and over, with plenty of self-evaluation and instruction along the way. Here are a few of the more basic skills, shared by chaplains, clergy, therapists, and even hostage negotiators. They're all about building trust and helping the other person open up about themselves.

Listen actively. When someone starts talking, we try to listen intently and show that we're engaged. A good rule is to listen to the person like they're speaking a language that you're familiar with but in which you are not quite fluent. That's the level of concentration and focus that active listening requires. Also start paying attention to how you listen generally. Do you interrupt? Do you formulate your response while the other person is still talking? Make your shopping list? Where are your eyes? Have someone tell you a story while you actively listen, and then try to tell it back to them. Also pay attention to how other people listen to you. You'll begin to appreciate how active listening is actually holy listening. It's a gift that conveys reverence and care for the person speaking and treats their words like a gift in themselves.

Reflect back what you hear. One way to show that you're listening and also understanding is to reflect or offer back to the speaker what you hear them say. This reflection allows the speaker to feel heard and verify that you've understood them correctly. It also builds trust and rapport and often leads the person to share more deeply. One technique is to summarize or paraphrase the main point of what you've just heard. You can also name the emotion that is not explicitly stated but that you pick up from the other person. "That sounds really frustrating" or "How exciting!" You can even parrot something the person just said nearly verbatim, perhaps with a question mark at the end. So if someone says, "I just wanted to go home," you can respond with, "You wanted to go home?" I know this technique might seem a little unnatural at first, but trust me: it works. All these techniques work, at least when done well. This revelation came as a shock to me initially. I remember thinking the whole idea of reflecting back was ridiculous, that patients would see right through it and laugh me out of the room. But the opposite was true. People opened right up, especially as I got more skilled. However, I did learn one important lesson along the way: don't act like a parrot too many times, or it *will* get weird.

Ask open-ended questions. Open-ended questions allow a person to provide whatever amount of detail they want rather than simply a one-word answer. They can lead someone to share relevant material about their life, way of thinking, and beliefs. The best questions are simple, brief, and to the point. "What do you like about your job?" or "How did you feel when that happened?" or "Can you say more?" Clarifying questions that start with "what," "why," and "how" encourage reflection and help the person get to the heart of things. Just be sure to pace your questions to allow some silence between the last answer and the next question. Questions that emerge too quickly can feel a little intrusive and cut off deeper insights and experiences of emotion. Sometimes a little attentive and thoughtful silence is all that's needed to invite the person to continue exploring the matter at hand.

You'll notice that none of the skills mentioned above has to do with religion or spirituality or faith. They're just designed to get people talking about themselves and meaningful parts of their lives. But let's face it: anything meaningful is spiritual. As mentioned earlier in this book, spirituality is simply about sacred connection:

connection to God, connection to others, and connection to self.

So let's kick it up a notch. Let's look at another skill that allows us to put faith on the table and explicitly highlight the holy once we've entered into the realm of meaningful conversation.

>>>>>>>>>>>>>

Here's another experience from my seminary days: Evangelism Bootcamp. This was the title of a weekend conference at Virginia Theological Seminary, which is located in Alexandria. After a mere three hours into the conference, all the participants were instructed to fan out over the DC area and strike up conversations with strangers. The point was to get people talking about spiritual matters and maybe even God or Jesus.

I admit that initiating conversation with strangers is not everyone's cup of tea. It can be intimidating, awkward, and just plain scary, even if you don't intend to talk about God. But not for those of us who signed up for Evangelism Bootcamp. With a name like that, what else can you expect? We were seminarians, clergy, and other ministry professionals who embraced the idea of "progressive evangelism," a term coined by my very best friend in seminary, Otis, who had organized the conference. Otis explained that progressive evangelism is not about getting people to come to church or believe in God. It's about revealing the presence of God already there in the person's life and in the midst of your conversation with them. Otis is brilliant at striking up a conversation with absolutely anyone. So before we set out, he made sure we discussed ways to talk to people in a way that feels natural. Comment on the person's shirt or how long the bus is taking to arrive. Ask about the book they're reading or whether the pastry they bought at the coffee shop is any good. Treat small talk as a door to a better and more interesting conversation—using all those pastoral care skills learned in CPE—and then get down to business. In this case, turning the conversation toward the divine. Like I said, anything meaningful is spiritual, so it's not as big of a jump to make as we sometimes assume.

This is where the stranger part doesn't make that much of a difference. Whether you're in a conversation with someone you know well or someone you don't know at all, you can do this one simple technique: name the holy. Name what you understand as the presence of God in what the person is saying. I learned this from David Gortner, a priest and professor who spoke at the bootcamp. He writes about naming the holy in his book *Transforming Evangelism*. Here are some examples I've used: "You seem really grounded. Do you have a spiritual side?" "I would say God has blessed you with a passion for teaching." "What you're describing doesn't sound like a mere coincidence. I wonder if God might have had something to do with it." "Everything came together in the last minute? That sounds like the God I know."

What I discovered in Evangelism Bootcamp, and have witnessed ever since, is that many people are genuinely interested in spiritual conversation. They are open to considering the holy in their lives and hearing about the holy in our lives too. Many of us just don't know how to start down that road toward spiritual conversation, or else we let our fear of being awkward or offending someone stop the conversation before it even starts. You could see these conversations as a form of relational evangelism, or you could see them as simply creating space for both parties to share their spiritual selves. Gortner writes, "Evangelism is a willful, joyful spiritual discipline of seeing and naming the Holy Spirit at work in ourselves and those we encounter—giving voice to our own grace-filled experiences, and helping others find their voice."

This means that whenever we seek to have a conversation about faith, we need to be prepared to speak to "our own grace-filled experiences." We must be ready to carry our side of the conversation in a way that not only testifies to the presence and power of God in our lives but connects with what the other person is saying.

Consider the idea of a spiritual library. We each have a library made up of various books that include our beliefs about God and our experiences of God. Books can include moments of awakening, times of hardship that led to growth, favorite Scriptures or hymns and why they're our favorite, and many other topics. A good exercise is to take stock of the books in your library and start honing your stories. Here are some prompts to get you going, including a few directly from Dr. Gortner:

- "Is there a principle by which you try to live your life? How did you come to believe that?"

- "Have you ever felt divided against yourself, acting or speaking in ways out of keeping with your deepest convictions? What happened?"
- "When has your heart stirred with an expansive love and desire to commit yourself to the good of others? What sparked that experience, and what did you do?"
- Reflect on doubts about faith, God, or the church that you've had during different seasons of life. How did you respond to those doubts? What sustained you?
- Have you ever sensed God moving you to do something or make a change in your life? What was it? What happened?

You might find that your spiritual library is pretty expansive and that it contains more resources than you'd initially thought. If you're familiar with what's in there, you'll be ready to pull a book off the shelf to share with someone else who could benefit from it.

Let's go back to chaplaincy for a moment. An important part about being an interfaith chaplain is that you don't focus on your personal faith beliefs. You focus on those of the patient. During my experience with hospital chaplaincy, I learned how to be a comfort to people in times of need and to be a sounding board for lamentation. I helped patients and family members make spiritual sense of what was going on. If someone asked me "Why did God let me get cancer?" my job was not to answer the question. My job was to help them answer the question for themselves in terms of their own religious beliefs and understanding of God.

But sometimes I was hit with a direct question that demanded a direct answer. "So. You think there's a heaven, huh?" a patient once asked me sarcastically, with a hint of fear in his voice. Another time the wife of a dying man challenged, "How can you watch him suffer like this and still believe in God?" It sounded like an accusation, but I think she was longing for some word of hope. Neither she nor the man inquiring about heaven was looking for a fight or asking for a scholarly argument. They wanted my testimony. And maybe they were even looking for the testimony of the church—the church that has stood in the midst of devastation and turmoil and made truly outlandish claims. "Christ is risen!" is one of them.

Testimony is publicly recognizing that you have seen light in the darkness, that you have felt love overcome fear, that you have met God. It's personal and firsthand, just like in a courtroom. When taking the stand, witnesses give their own testimony but aren't allowed to speak for others—that would be hearsay. I don't remember what testimony I gave to the people in the hospital, but I'm pretty sure it wasn't elaborate or lengthy. In fact, it was probably as simple as "I do believe in heaven. And I believe we'll both be there one day."

The examples from the hospital might seem a little extreme. But I bet we all have a book in our spiritual libraries that contains our thoughts on the afterlife. We all have a book about finding God in the midst of suffering. The specific content we draw from our books, and how we go about sharing what we find in their pages, is driven by context. Talking about heaven to someone who is actively dying is certainly different than pondering what heaven is like over drinks with a friend.

There are a host of other factors to consider as well when initiating a sacred conversation. What is the other person's emotional state? Are they a person of faith? Do the two of you have shared life experience? Do the two of you have shared knowledge of the Bible?

The point isn't to find the exact right thing to say. The point is to be bold enough to open one of our spiritual books when we believe it can serve someone else—whether that person is a stranger or a friend, someone with a deep faith or no faith at all. What we offer doesn't have to be eloquent or well-constructed, just sincere. I love it when someone evangelizes to me in this way. Sharing our spiritual selves is a way of sharing God's grace.

》》》》》》》》》》

My first street prayer ministry was not "Ask me for a blessing." It wasn't even Ashes to Go. It was "Want Prayer?" I was in seminary at the time. I had purchased a rather flimsy A-frame sign from Staples and had "Want Prayer?" printed on it in large block letters. Scattered around the question "Want Prayer?" were additional words in smaller letters: family, employment, health, relationships, thanksgiving, and a few more that I don't remember.

I stood with my sign in the mall, outside the city library, and at the occasional town festival in and around Stamford, Connecticut. Otis, whom you'll remember from Evangelism Bootcamp, stood with me. Putting yourself out there can be a little easier with a partner. I imagine this is one reason Jesus sent out his disciples two by two.

My experience with "Want Prayer?" bore many similarities to "Ask me for a blessing." The primary difference was that nearly everyone who stopped at my "Want Prayer?" station was a Christian. They seemed to know the drill of having someone pray for them out loud. Many would reach for my hand and bow their heads or lift their chins upward with eyes closed. Some even interjected "Yes, Lord!" or "Amen!" or "Mmh!" throughout the prayer. Others were considerably more subdued but, on the whole, quite comfortable with receiving prayer—in *public*, which is no small thing. It takes a certain boldness to ask for prayer, just like it takes a certain boldness to offer it.

Much like Evangelism Bootcamp, street prayer ministry is not for everyone. But praying out loud for another person can be. Of course, that doesn't make it easy. I've heard that public speaking is the greatest fear among Americans. I imagine that, for Christians, praying out loud is a close second. Most Christians I know are reticent about praying aloud for anyone or anything if it means they have to come up with something to say off the top of their heads. Ask for a volunteer to open a Bible study or church meeting in prayer? Crickets. That's why I often seek a volunteer in advance. That way the person has time to select an appropriate prayer from our Episcopal prayer book or another source, or maybe write their own prayer. This is a great first step in getting comfortable praying aloud.

The next step is extemporaneous prayer—prayer that is unprepared or impromptu. It's an exercise in trusting the Holy Spirit to flow through you and inspire your words. Extemporaneous prayer is what we use when we pray for others on the spot or off the cuff. In some Christian traditions, sharing immediate needs and praying for one another in this way is a common thing to do.

However, it can be intimidating even for those familiar with this practice. Here are some pointers.

Pray out loud when you're alone. Voicing our normally silent prayers to God, when we're by ourselves, helps us focus and become more articulate while not having to worry about what we sound like to others. It's a low-pressure situation that helps us build confidence. Try looking at pictures of loved ones and praying aloud for each one.

Keep it short and sweet. Prayer doesn't need to be long for God to hear it or for another person to be moved by it. A brief, heartfelt prayer is plenty powerful. If you've had a conversation leading up to prayer, you might have more information about the person's concern and more things to lift up to God. Even so, there is no need for flowery or super-spiritual language that doesn't feel natural.

If you want to be prepared with a plan or framework for your prayer, consider this: (1) Start by addressing God with an affirmation about God's character or how God acts in the world. If you can relate it to what the person has told you, all the better. If someone wants prayer for a sick loved one, for example, you might say, "Jesus, you are our Great Physician." (2) Throw in some thanks. Thanking God often comes naturally to us and is appropriate to include in any type of prayer. You can offer a thanksgiving that relates to the person's prayer request or the way that you've just addressed God: "Thank you for your healing love and your healing touch." You can connect it to the other person, especially if you know them: "Thank you for Andrew and his desire to seek and serve you." Or you can keep it general: "Thank you for this opportunity to come before you in prayer." (3) Then offer the reason for the prayer: "Please be with Amanda as she undergoes surgery tomorrow. Pour out your presence and peace upon her and guide the doctors' hands. Give her a full recovery and restore her to health and wholeness." (4) Close your prayer in the name of God, Jesus, or the Trinity (Father, Son, and Holy Spirit).

Practice, practice, practice. At first, praying aloud might feel forced or awkward. God doesn't mind, and chances are the person you're praying for doesn't either. The best way to feel and sound more comfortable is to keep doing it. With practice, you'll move from being nervous to relaxed, and you'll find yourself becoming a conduit of God's grace more and more, blessing the person you're with and blessing God with your prayers.

Praying out loud can be a gentle and earnest form of evangelism. It's not just about what we say in our prayers for others but the loving intention behind the prayers themselves. When someone prays for you in a way that is sincere and pure, you can feel that person's love come through and touch your heart. It becomes mixed with God's love and attests to God's power to heal, strengthen, and renew.

In case you didn't notice, these lessons from a seminarian are not lessons from a priest. In other words, I learned them all before becoming a clergyperson. This means that you don't have to be ordained, or be a ministry professional with years of experience, to put them into practice. Blessing others, specifically through spiritual conversation and prayer, is something we can all do. And it's something the world needs, including the people in your life—your spouse, your neighbor, your friend from church, perhaps even the stranger you meet in line at the post office. So what do you think? Want to try it? God's grace is meant to be shared.

EPILOGUE

I've been doing these stints on the sidewalk roughly once a week for five years, and it's rare that I get fewer than five people who ask for a blessing during a given morning. Two was my lowest number . . . until the day I got exactly zero takers.

It was a crisp and clear spring day. Beautiful and sunny. It was pre-pandemic, so I certainly couldn't blame the coronavirus for keeping people away. Maybe I was having a bad hair day? Whatever the reason, I got plenty of smiles, nods, the occasional "good morning," and even a thumbs up, but not one person who stopped.

It was a blow, I have to admit. I was feeling a little sorry for myself as I waited out the last few minutes of my half-hour shift. Then a dog walked up to my "Ask me for a blessing" sign, lifted his hind leg up next to the chalkboard, and peed. He even managed to wash off some of the lettering. It was a very quick mark of territory, and the owner seemed too stunned to pull his dog away. He mumbled something unintelligible and hurried on, clearly embarrassed.

Then again, maybe it was only unintelligible because I was laughing so loudly. God must have been telling me to lighten up, and it had worked. No pity parties allowed in this line of work.

The next week, I was out there again, and a woman told me, "I saw you last Tuesday and was too timid to say anything; I'm glad you're back." Then she proceeded to tell me her prayer request. This is not an uncommon occurrence. The consistency of offering blessings at the same time, in the same place, week after week allows people to warm up to the idea of talking to me before actually doing it. So I'm not surprised when someone says they've seen me here before.

That said, the next person who stopped caught me totally off guard. It was the guy with the dog! I'm not sure I would have recognized either of them had they kept on walking. But he felt the need to apologize, which gave us a chance to laugh and chat. Then he told me how much he appreciated the church's flag hanging right above us. It has a large cross and the verse Matthew 28:20: "I am with you always." It's a beautiful reminder of Jesus's ongoing presence in the world, in our hearts, and by our sides. I imagine many, many people have drawn comfort and strength from that flag as they've passed by the church. Even after looking up at it hundreds of times, I still do.

Once the man and his dog had moved along, I thought about how God uses us even when we don't realize it. The sight of someone or something bearing witness to God's love can lift another person's spirits and encourage their faith. So what if I have a day when no one asks me for a blessing? Just being out there might be enough. If even one person sees me with my weather-beaten, peed-on sign and thinks, *Oh, how nice*, or, better yet, *Maybe I'll pray today*, then, well, to God be the glory.

May the same be true for you. As you bear witness to God's love—through blessing others in word and deed and in ways you don't even realize—may you always know that you are a vessel of God's grace. And the blessing of God Almighty, the Father, the Son, and the Holy Spirit, be upon you and remain with you always.

ACKNOWLEDGMENTS

Ask Me for a Blessing—both the ministry and the book—would not exist without Otis Gaddis, my forever favorite partner in evangelism and closest spiritual friend. Otis, I owe you so much. You not only helped me find my voice for this particular form of spiritual outreach; you helped me find my voice in the Episcopal Church. I will be eternally grateful to you and all our friends who made up the Episcopal Evangelism Network—the best part of seminary by far.

To my former boss, Doug Ousley, who let me bring this ministry to the Church of the Incarnation and even blessed people one Tuesday in my absence. I know this is not your usual cup of tea and love the fact that you got out there anyway and felt surprisingly blessed when you did.

To my boss before Doug, Brenda Husson, who let me bring Ashes to Go and then Blessings to Go to St. James' Church, and our clergy colleagues who joined in: Craig Townsend, Will Peyton, and Ryan Fleenor. The ways you supported me as a new priest and your clear love of Jesus continue to inspire me to this day. I was blessed to be part of such an awesome clergy team.

To all the people I've blessed on the sidewalk, from parishioners, to new acquaintances and friends, to strangers I'll never see again. Your stories are truly sacred, and to bring your needs before God together is one of the greatest honors of my life.

To John Sargent for being so generous with your time, counsel, and encouragement when I knew nothing about writing a book.

To my editor, Valerie Weaver-Zercher, for "discovering" me and shepherding me through this entire process, from book proposal to publication. You are a treasure, and I hope to work together again.

To my spiritual director, Sister Marylin Gramas, whose guidance and wisdom show up in these pages because they've so richly enhanced my understanding, experience, and sharing of God's love.

Finally, thank you to my family for cheering me on every step of the way. To my parents, siblings, and in-laws, who have celebrated and shared my writing, even when I knew it needed work. To my daughter, Callaway, who has taught me so much about God—one of the reasons she makes so many appearances in this book. And most importantly, to my husband, Jess, who makes life beautiful. You called me an author before anyone else did and helped me see not only what this book could become but who I am in it. Your vision is a spiritual gift, and you are my greatest love. I couldn't be prouder to be your wife as we look to a bright future of new possibilities, endeavors, and adventures with God.

NOTES

CHAPTER 1

3 *"According to all three"*: Jeffrey M. Jones, "U.S. Church Membership Falls Below Majority for First Time," Gallup Politics, March 29, 2021, https://news.gallup.com/poll/341963/church-membership-falls-below-majority-first-time.aspx; "In U.S., Decline of Christianity Continues at Rapid Pace," Pew Research Center, October 17, 2019, https://www.pewforum.org/2019/10/17/in-u-s-decline-of-christianity-continues-at-rapid-pace/; "A Snapshot of Faith Practice Across Age Groups," Barna Group, July 23, 2019, https://www.barna.com/research/faithview-on-faith-practice/.

3 *"And while plenty of cities are considered"*: "The Most Post-Christian Cities in America: 2019," Barna Group, June 5, 2019, https://www.barna.com/research/post-christian-cities-2019/.

13 *"This, in turn, can affect a person's connection"*: Kim Tingley, "We Need to Understand the Difference Between Isolation and Loneliness," *New York Times Magazine*, August 18, 2021, https://www.nytimes.com/2021/08/18/magazine/isolation-loneliness-health.html.

18 *"As God told Abraham"*: See Genesis 12:2–3.

19 *"The prayer of a righteous person"*: James 5:16 (NIV).

CHAPTER 2

32 *"God's favor toward us, unearned and undeserved"*: Episcopal Church, *Book of Common Prayer and Administration of the Sacraments and Other Rites and Ceremonies of the Church: Together with the Psalter or Psalms of David According to the Use of the Episcopal Church* (New York: Seabury Press, 1979), 857.

41 *"Outward and visible signs of an inward and spiritual grace"*: *Book of Common Prayer*, 857.

41 *"Union with Christ in his death and resurrection"*: *Book of Common Prayer*, 858.

42 *"You are sealed by the Holy Spirit in baptism"*: *Book of Common Prayer*, 308.

42 *"That neither death, nor life, nor angels, nor rulers"*: Romans 8:38–39.

CHAPTER 3

52 *"Every generous act of giving"*: James 1:17.

55 *"Humble yourselves before the Lord"*: James 4:10.

61 *"Whenever I am weak, then I am strong"*: 2 Corinthians 2:10.

CHAPTER 4

76 *"Approach the throne of grace with boldness"*: Hebrews 4:16.

78 *"I have been crucified with Christ"*: Galatians 2:19.

81 *"Finally, beloved, whatever is true"*: Philippians 4:8.

82 *"And though I am in no way religious"*: Tony Shea, "Let's Get Our Dogs Blessed, Shall We?," *Shea Magazine*, https://sheamagazine.com/lets-get-dogs-blessed-shall/.

86 *"We are not worthy"*: Book of Common Prayer, p. 337.

87 *"I don't believe Jesus needs to protect us from God"*: See Hosea 13:8.

95 *"Father, through Jesus Christ your Son"*: Book of Common Prayer, 533.

97 *"Bless those who curse you"*: Luke 6:28.

CHAPTER 5

106 *"Go tell John what you hear and see"*: Matthew 11:4–6.

111–112 *"A sword will pierce your own soul too"*: Luke 2:35.

112 *"Her cousin Elizabeth calls her blessed"*: See Luke 1:48, 42.

114 *"The Beatitudes appear in the Gospels of Luke and Matthew"*: See Luke 6:20–22; Matthew 5:3–12.

119 *"blessed are you who are poor"*: Luke 6:20.

119 *"Indeed, it is easier for a camel to go through"*: Luke 18:25.

126 *"Power at work within us is able to accomplish"*: Ephesians 3:20.

128 *"Everything exposed by the light becomes visible"*: Ephesians 5:13–14.

CHAPTER 6

132 *"The Almighty and merciful Lord grant you absolution"*: Book of Common Prayer, 42.

139 *"For he will command his angels concerning you"*: Psalm 91:11–12.

146 *"The Spirit of the Lord is upon me"*: Luke 4:18.

148 *"Unequally yoked"*: 2 Corinthians 6:14.

151 *"Confess him with a quiet confidence"*: Philippians 2:11.

154 *"With sighs too deep for words"*: Romans 8:26.

154 *"I believe; help my unbelief!"* Mark 9:24.

157 *"Whoever dwells in the shelter of the Most High"*: Psalm 91:1 (NIV).

CHAPTER 7

170 *"Evangelism is a willful, joyful spiritual discipline":* David Gortner, *Transforming Evangelism* (New York: Church Publishing, 2008), 32.

170 *"Is there a principle":* Gortner, *Transforming Evanglism,* 136.

171 *"Have you ever felt divided against yourself":* Gortner, *Transforming Evangelism,* 129.

171 *"When has your heart stirred":* Gortner, *Transforming Evangelism,* 128.

171 *"Reflect on doubts about faith":* The inspiration for this prompt comes from a participant's worksheet from the Women of the Evangelical Lutheran Church in America, *The Witness of Women: An Evangelism Strategy* (Chicago: Women of the Evangelical Lutheran Church in America, 1994).